Volumetric Image Analysis

Volumetric Image Analysis

Gabriele Lohmann

Max-Planck Institute of Cognitive Neuroscience
Leipzig, Germany

WILEY TEUBNER

A Partnership between John Wiley & Sons and B. G. Teubner Publishers

Chichester · New York · Weinheim · Brisbane · Toronto · Singapore · Stuttgart · Leipzig

John Wiley & Sons Ltd
Baffins Lane
Chichester
West Sussex
PO19 1UD
England

B.G. Teubner
Industriestraße 15
70565 Stuttgart (Vaihingen)
Postfach 80 10 69
70510 Stuttgart
Germany

National Chichester 01243 779777
International (+44) 1243 779777

National Stuttgart (0711) 789010
International (+49) 711 789010

e-mail (for orders and customer service enquiries): cs-books@wiley.co.uk
Visit our Home Page on http://www.wiley.co.uk or http://www.wiley.com

Other Wiley Editorial Offices

John Wiley & Sons, Inc., 605 Third Avenue, New York, NY 10158-0012, USA

Weinheim · Brisbane · Singapore · Toronto

Other Teubner Editorial Offices

B.G. Teubner, Verlagsgesellschaft mbH, Johannisgasse 16, D-04103 Leipzig, Germany

Die Deutsche Bibliothek—CIP-Einheitsaufnahme

Lohmann, Gabriele:
Volumetric image analysis / Gabriele Lohmann.-
Chichester; New York; Brisbane; Toronto; Singapore;
Stuttgart; Leipzig: Wiley-Teubner, 1998
    ISBN 3 519 06447 2 (Teubner)
    ISBN 0 471 96785 8 (Wiley)

British Library Cataloguing in Publication Data

A catalogue record for this book is available from the British Library

ISBN 0 471 96785 8
ISBN Teubner 3 519 06447 2

Produced from PostScript files supplied by the author
Printed and bound in Great Britain by Biddles Ltd, Guildford and King's Lynn
This book is printed on acid-free paper responsibly manufactured from sustainable forestry in which at least two trees are planted for each one used for paper production.

Contents

Preface

Volumetric digital images are three-dimensional image arrays corresponding to a stack of two-dimensional slices, produced for instance by a tomographic scanner. Such images play an important role in various applications, especially in medical image processing, in the processing of seismic data and in many other domains.

While the automatic analysis of two-dimensional images has received a lot of attention for a number of years now, interest in the analysis of three-dimensional images was dormant for a long time. However, things have changed decidedly in recent years, which is partly due to the fact that new scanner technology has become available providing massive amounts of volumetric data. At the same time, advances in computer technology have made it possible to handle these large amounts of data. As a result, a wealth of new algorithms for the analysis of volumetric images has been developed and put to use.

I believe that the time has now come to bring these various techniques into a coherent form and present them as a textbook. While a large number of excellent textbooks about the analysis of 2D images are available today, a textbook on the analysis of 3D images was lacking up to now. I hope that this book will help to fill the void.

There are a number of issues that are specific to the analysis of volumetric image data. Volumetric images are usually much larger than two-dimensional images and thus call for space efficient analysis techniques. Furthermore, differences between two- and three-dimensional geometry stand in the way of a straightforward generalization from the two-dimensional to the three-dimensional case.

This book presents a largely self-contained comprehensive introduction to the field in a form that can serve as a textbook at the senior/graduate level. It will also be useful to engineers and computer scientists with an interest in developing volumetric image analysis systems. In addition, users of such systems may find it helpful as a reference.

Acknowledgements

I could not have written this book without the support I have received from a number of people. In particular, I would like to thank Professor Dr. D. Yves von Cramon, director at the Max-Planck-Institute of Cognitive Neuroscience in Leipzig, and Professor Dr. Bernd Radig of the Computer Science department at the Technical University of Munich. Special thanks are also due to my colleague Dr. Frithjof Kruggel who has been supportive throughout.

A number students of the Computer Science department of the Technical University of Munich have helped in the preparation of this book, either by writing their Diploma thesis on a topic related to a chapter of the book or by doing a lab project. My thanks goes to the following students: Michael Haubner, Alexander Seidel, Michael Erskine, Markus Laux, Markus Holeczek, Christof Kaleschke, Lars Klawitter, Günter Heiß, Werner Krötz, Dirk Nitsche, Peter Zoller, Peter Schickel, Andreas Rier, Thomas Höller, Alfred Dietel, Winfried Dietmayer and Doris Reisenauer.

A particularly bothersome task connected with the production of any book is proof-reading and error checking, in which several of my colleagues at the Max-Planck-Institute of Cognitive Neuroscience were exceedingly helpful, in particular Dr. Xavier Descombes, Dr. Jagath and Menaka Rajapakse, Dr. Christian Uhl, Ulrich Hartmann and Jan Kowalski. I should hasten to add that any remaining errors are of course entirely my fault.

Last but not least, I would like to thank the people from both John Wiley & Sons, Publishers and Teubner Verlag, Stuttgart, in particular Dr. Jens Schlembach and Christian Rauscher.

Chapter 1

Introduction

Digital volumetric images are stacks of two-dimensional image slices. We can think of these slices as serial cross-sections through a scene depicting objects in a digitized three-dimensional world. Such images play an important role in many different areas of application, most notably in medical imaging but also in geology and many other domains.

In computed tomography (CT) for instance, three-dimensional images are obtained as reconstructions from projections produced by a fan of X-ray beams. Magnetic resonance tomography (MRT) is another source of volumetric images. In microscopy, volumetric images are acquired as serial cross-sections through some object of interest so that each cross-section represents one image slice.

Other sources of volumetric images are for instance some types of ultrasound imaging, and so-called *range images*. A single range image is a two-dimensional image, in which each pixel records the distance between the viewer's position and the nearest object in the scene. If several range images are taken from various directions, they can be compiled into a 3D data set. Time sequences of 2D images may also be thought of as being three-dimensional images in which the time axis constitutes the third dimension. There are a number of issues that are specific to the analysis of time sequences which will however not be addressed in this book.

Two-dimensional images are composed of *picture elements* or *pixels* for short, while the building blocks of three-dimensional images are *volume elements* or *voxels*. Typically, a volumetric image contains dozens or even hundreds of image slices each slice being an array of voxels.

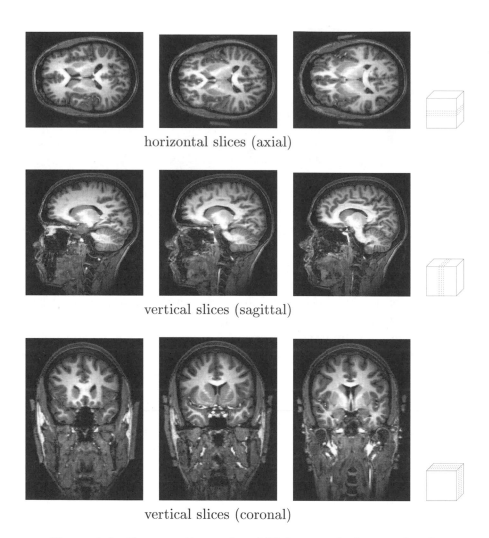

horizontal slices (axial)

vertical slices (sagittal)

vertical slices (coronal)

Figure 1.1: Cross-sections of an MR image of a human head

Slices in volumetric images need not be viewed in the orientation in which they were originally acquired. In fact, one may think of a volumetric image as a cube that may be cut into serial slices in any of the three orthogonal directions aligned with the cube's faces. Figure 1.1 illustrates this idea. It shows a few slices of a magnetic resonance image of a human head viewed in each of the three orthogonal directions.

Image analysis in general aims at several objectives: in the easiest case, we want to prepare an image for visualization or for subsequently more elaborate processing by performing noise cleaning or contrast enhancement.

A more difficult task is to geometrically align two or more different images so that comparisons between them become possible. To achieve good results, we often have to perform a number of preparatory steps prior to the actual registration procedure. For instance, we may first have to extract landmarks such as salient lines or points from our image data which help to guide the alignment process.

This brings us to the next major goal of image analysis, namely the automatic extraction of structures from the image data. Consider for instance the image in figure 1.1 depicting a human head. Suppose we want to investigate brain anatomy on the basis of this data. We will first have to extract the brain by removing any non-brain tissue from the image – a process which is sometimes called "brain peeling", and which will be discussed in section 8.3. Clearly, brain peeling is only the first step after which other image analysis routines follow.

The most advanced goal of image analysis is *image understanding* which involves attaching a symbolic label to the structures that were extracted, so that the image content is represented at a very high level of abstraction.

The analysis of two-dimensional images has received a lot of attention during recent decades. Correspondingly, a large number of excellent textbooks are available today, for example [1], [2], [3], [4], to name just a few.

In contrast, interest in the analysis of three-dimensional images was dormant until some time ago. However, things have changed dramatically in recent years, which is partly due to the fact that new scanner technology has become available providing massive amounts of 3D data [5]. At the same time, the advance of computer technology has made the handling of large data sets feasible. 3D data sets are often much

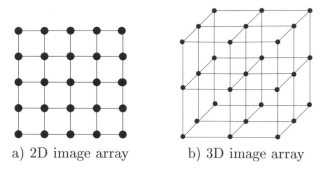

a) 2D image array   b) 3D image array

Figure 1.2: Adjacency in 2D and in 3D

larger than 2D image data sets, so fast computers with lots of internal memory are required for the processing.

The focus of this book is the analysis of three-dimensional image data. Let us now discuss differences in the analysis of two- and three-dimensional data. Perhaps the most important difference is induced by differences between two- and three-dimensional topology. Consider for instance some object depicted in a digital image. In 2D, the boundary delineating this object can be easily traced by a "right-hand-on-wall" strategy, in which we walk around the object so that the interior always remains to the right until we reach the starting point again.

In 3D however, an object's boundary is defined by a surface which separates the interior from the exterior, and there is no obvious strategy for tracing a surface. Thus, object boundaries have quite different properties in 3D than in 2D. A large portion of this book is therefore devoted to the handling of surfaces in images.

Spatial adjacency within an image array also depends on the dimensionality. Consider figure 1.2. Each pixel in the two-dimensional array is adjacent to at most eight other pixels, whereas in the 3D array, each voxel may have up to twenty-six neighbours depending on our definition of adjacency. This has a number of interesting consequences which will be discussed in due course.

Note that volumetric images inherently represent the spatial relations within a scene. In contrast, two-dimensional images represent two-dimensional projections of three-dimensional scenes which heavily depend on the viewpoint from which the images were acquired. Consequently, a large part of the analysis of two-dimensional images is devoted to recovering spatial structure from such projections. Luckily, problems induced by viewpoint dependency do not arise in our context, and will therefore not be discussed.

This book focuses on the presentation of basic methods for the analysis of volumetric images. We will not primarily present complete solutions to practical problems (although occasionally this may happen as well). Instead, we will present basic tools which are fundamental and ubiquitous in our context. Such basic methods are characterized by the fact that they offer solutions to *generic problems* such as surface detection or curvature computation which may appear in many different tasks. Generally, solutions to practical problems are obtained by applying several such basic methods in sequence.

As noted above, there are a number of such generic problems that are specific to the analysis of volumetric images. On the other hand, some image analysis methods easily generalize from 2D to 3D. We will present some of these methods anyhow, especially if they are essential for making this book self-contained. In those cases, we will only give a coarse outline. References to the literature for further reading will be given instead. Methods specific to 3D will be presented at a much higher level of detail.

This book is organized into three parts. The first part specifically addresses the analysis of volumetric *binary* images, i.e. images whose voxels are either black or white, so that no intermediate shades of grey occur. We begin by presenting the basic concepts of discrete topology such as the problem of spatial adjacency as introduced above. We then move on to connected component analysis, feature extraction in binary images and conclude this part by presenting several operations defined on binary images.

The second part discusses the analysis of volumetric *grey level* images. We begin with simple image enhancement methods, before we come to geometric transformations. The automatic extraction of surfaces and other structures from volumetric images is the main focus of this part.

The third part presents methods for object modelling and registration. The main point here is that once structures have been successfully extracted using any of the methods presented in the first two parts, we need to represent them at a higher level of abstraction to make them accessible to either image understanding tasks or to prepare them for visualization.

Some topics are presented only very briefly. This is especially true for visualization methods. We have deliberately kept the presentation of such methods short for two reasons. Firstly, the subject is so large that it is clearly beyond the scope of this book. Secondly, many excellent textbooks already exist on the subject of computer graphics to which the interested reader should refer.

Part I

3D Binary Images

Chapter 2

Basics

2.1 Basic definitions

In this section, we will present some basic definitions and notational conventions which will be used throughout this book. We begin by defining terms relating to digital images composed of individual picture elements and proceed to define adjacency relationships within such images.

n-dimensional digital images can be thought of as n-dimensional arrays of grey values such that each array element represents exactly one picture point. Array elements of two-dimensional images are called *pixels (picture elements)* and elements of three-dimensional arrays are called *voxels (volume elements)*. General n-dimensional array elements are also called *raster elements*. In some texts they are called *spatial elements* or *spels* for short.

Each such raster element encodes the "colour" or the shade of grey present at the corresponding location within the image by a numerical code called a *grey code*. Usually, grey codes are given as integers ranging from 0 to 255 where the code value of 0 represents the colour "black" and the code 255 represents "white" while intermediate grey codes represent various shades of grey. The reason why the set $\{i \mid i = 0, 1, 2, ..., 255\}$ is frequently used for grey codes is that every element of this set can be stored in one byte, as one byte consists of eight bits and can thus be used to store up to $2^8 = 256$ different entities. Sometimes, greater

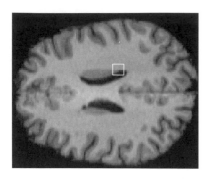

166	176	169	164	166	167	164	167
170	171	169	168	168	163	164	166
170	168	172	170	174	162	165	168
165	165	169	165	173	161	163	164
155	154	154	149	151	134	133	130
141	136	128	117	98	57	59	54
128	118	94	69	45	36	37	28
91	78	57	45	38	39	31	25

Figure 2.1: A digital image and its grey codes

accuracy in representing grey values is required so that other sets of grey codes such as the set of real numbers ranging from 0 to 1 must be used. Figure 2.1 shows an example of a two-dimensional digital image and a small window of its corresponding image matrix.

In this first part of the book, we will talk about image analysis algorithms that expect *binary images* as input and produce output images that are often but not always also binary.

In this chapter, we will concentrate on *binary images*, i.e. images whose set of grey codes is given by the set $\{0, 1\}$. We can think of such images as black-and-white images showing no intermediate shades of grey. Raster elements whose grey codes are equal to "0" can be thought of as being "switched off", and are usually depicted in white, whereas raster elements whose grey code is equal to "1" are "switched on", and are depicted as black.

Unfortunately, this convention is inconsistent with the conventions we described in the beginning of this chapter. Remember that for grey code images whose grey code set was $\{0, ..., 255\}$ the grey code "0" represented "black" and not "white" as for binary images. We will nonetheless adhere to this convention as it is widely used.

The subset of "black" voxels within an image is usually assumed to depict some object, and therefore black voxels are deemed to belong to the image's *foreground*, whereas "white" voxels depict the image's *background*. In the context of binary images we will use the terms "foreground" and "black" synonymously, likewise the terms "background" and "white".

Figure 2.2 shows three different visualizations of the same two-

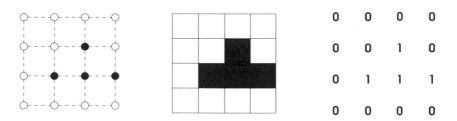

Figure 2.2: Three visualizations of a 4×4 binary image matrix

dimensional binary image matrix. In the following, we will alternatively use any one of these three representations.

Three-dimensional images can be thought of as a stack of two-dimensional image arrays. Each such two-dimensional array that helps to form a three-dimensional image is called a *slice*. We usually index these slices from top to bottom so that the top slice is numbered "0", the next slice is numbered "1", and so forth.

The set of addresses is sometimes referred to as the *image lattice*. More precisely, the image lattice is the set:

$$\{(s, r, c) \mid 0 \leq s < nslices, 0 \leq r < nrows, 0 \leq c < ncolumns\}$$

where *nslices*, *nrows*, *ncolumns* denote the number of slices, rows and columns.

Likewise, we will index rows and columns within each slice so that each raster element is associated with a unique raster address given as a (slice, row, column)-triplet in the three dimensions or a (row-column)-pair in two dimensions. Thus, voxels can be formally represented as

$$v_{s,r,c} \in G$$

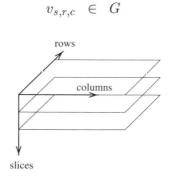

Figure 2.3: A stack of slices

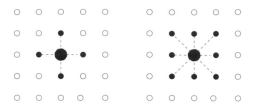

Figure 2.4: 4 and 8 adjacent neighbours

where G represents the set of grey codes, and s, r, c denotes the raster address. Likewise, two-dimensional pixels are denoted as $p_{r,c} \in G$.

An n-tuple representing a raster address is sometimes also called a *lattice point*.

Whenever possible we will subsequently display image arrays so that columns are indexed from left to right, and rows are indexed either from front to back or from top to bottom, depending on whether we display a stack of slices or a single slice. Figure 2.3 illustrates this arrangement.

2.1.1 Connectivity

So far we have looked at individual raster elements irrespective of their location within the image lattice. Let us now describe adjacency relationships within such a lattice. For simplicity, let us assume that an image lattice of infinite size is given so that we do not need to worry about image borders.

Let us begin with the two-dimensional case. First note that in 2D each pixel has four immediate neighbours whose raster addresses differ in at most one coordinate. In addition, there are four diagonal neighbours whose coordinates differ in both places as shown in figure 2.4.

The set of the four nearest neighbours is called the *4-neighbourhood* of the centre pixel, and the set of the eight nearest neighbours that comprises the 4-neighbourhood plus the additional four diagonal neighbours is called the *8-neighbourhood* of the centre pixel.

In three dimensions, each voxel has six neighbouring voxels whose raster addresses differ in at most one coordinate. In addition, there are twelve voxels whose addresses differ in exactly two coordinates and another eight voxels whose addresses differ in all three coordinates. Correspondingly, there are three different types of neighbourhood system in three dimensions (see figure 2.5).

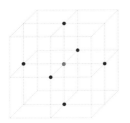 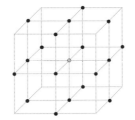 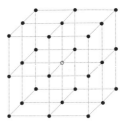

a) 6-neighbourhood   b) 18-neighbourhood   c) 26-neighbourhood

Figure 2.5: Neighbourhoods

Let us now formalize the concept of a neighbourhood a little further. Clearly, the concept of distances between raster elements is crucial. We will therefore define a metric on the image lattice that will allow us to measure distances between lattice points.

Definition 2.1 Let $x = (x_0, x_1, ..., x_n) \in Z^n$ and $y = (y_0, y_1, ..., y_n) \in Z^n$ be two points on an n-dimensional image lattice. The *Euclidean distance* between x and y is defined as:

$$D_0(x, y) = \sqrt{\sum_{i=1}^{n}(y_i - x_i)^2}.$$

The D_1-*distance* between x and y is defined as:

$$D_1(x, y) = \sum_{i=1}^{n}|y_i - x_i|$$

and the *max-distance* between x and y is defined as:

$$D_\infty(x, y) = \max_{i=1,...,n}|y_i - x_i|$$

Figure 2.6 shows the Euclidean distance and the D_1-distance between two points on a two-dimensional lattice. Note that the D_1-distance is always larger than the Euclidean distance.

The above definition allows us to reformulate neighbourhood systems more formally.

Definition 2.2 Let $x = (x_0, ..., x_n)$ be some point on an image lattice. The V_1^i neighbourhood of x is defined as

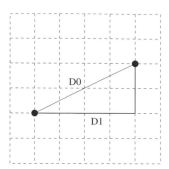

Figure 2.6: Distances on a discrete lattice

$$V_1^i(x) \;=\; \{y \mid D_1(x,y) \le i\}$$

and the V_∞^i neighbourhood of x is defined as

$$V_\infty^i(x) \;=\; \{y \mid D_\infty(x,y) \le i\}.$$

These neighbourhoods determine the set of lattice points within a radius of i from the centre point. Our earlier definitions of two-dimensional neighbourhoods now read as follows.

Definition 2.3 Let $x = (x_0, x_1)$ be some point on a two-dimensional image lattice. The n-neighbourhoods of x, $n = 4, 8$ are defined as follows:

$$
\begin{aligned}
N_4(x) &= V_1^1(x), \\
N_8(x) &= V_\infty^1(x).
\end{aligned}
$$

Likewise, let $x = (x_0, x_1, x_2)$ be some point on a three-dimensional image lattice. The n-neighbourhoods of x, $n = 6, 18, 26$ are defined as follows:

$$
\begin{aligned}
N_6(x) &= V_1^1(x) \\
N_{18}(x) &= V_1^2(x) \cap V_\infty^1(x) \\
N_{26}(x) &= V_\infty^1(x)
\end{aligned}
$$

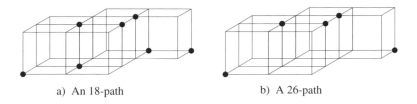

a) An 18-path   b) A 26-path

Figure 2.7: Discrete paths in a 3D lattice

If the centre voxel is to be excluded, we use the following notation:

$$N_k^*(x) = N_k(x) - \{x\}, \ k \in \{4, 6, 8, 18, 26\}$$

Remember that we can think of black voxels as belonging to an image "foreground" depicting one or several objects. Thus, black voxels are grouped together to form an object. In the following, we will present some definitions that will help us to address such groups of voxels.

Definition 2.4 Two points x, y are said to be *n-adjacent*, iff both points are n-neighbours of one another, i.e. iff $x \in N_n(y)$.

Definition 2.5 An *n-path* is a sequence of lattice points $(x_0, ..., x_{k-1})$ that are pairwise n-adjacent, i.e. x_i is n-adjacent to x_{i+1} for $i = 0, ..., k - 2$. An n-path $x_i, i = 0, ..., k - 1$ is said to be *closed*, iff $x_0 = x_{k-1}$.

Definition 2.6 A set $X \subset Z^d, d = 2, 3$ is called *n-connected* – or an *n-component* – if for any two points in X there is an n-path in X between these two points.

Usually, we consider either the components of the image foreground or the background. To distinguish between the two we sometimes talk of

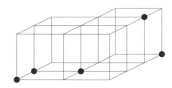

Figure 2.8: Three 6-components, two 18-components, and one 26-component

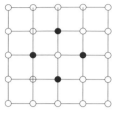 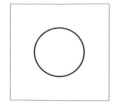

a) A closed digital 8-path   b) A closed continuous path

Figure 2.9: The Jordan theorem paradox

black components versus *white components*. Clearly, the number of components depends critically on the type of neighbourhood that we use. For instance, the foreground in figure 2.8 contains three 6-connected components, two 18-components and one 26-component.

Note that our definitions of adjacency and connectivity apply to black and white raster elements alike. However, this does not mean that we should employ the same type of connectivity for both foreground and background. In fact, we would run into serious trouble if we did. To see why, imagine some closed 8-path in a two-dimensional image such as the one shown in figure 2.9a. If we used 8-adjacency for both foreground and background in this case, foreground and background would form a single 8-connected component each.

This is quite awkward as we would expect a closed foreground path to completely enclose a connected component of the background thus separating the enclosed part of the background from the exterior part, so that the background would consist of two separate components rather than just one.

Figure 2.9b shows the corresponding continuous case. In continuous images, this problem does not arise. A closed continuous curve always separates the interior from the exterior part of the background. This fact is known as the *Jordan theorem* [6], [7].

Unfortunately, the discrete version of the Jordan theorem does not hold if we assume the same connectivity for both background and foreground. A simple way to avoid this problem is to adopt different connectivities. As the interior background pixel is not 4-connected to the exterior part of the background, there are two 4-connected background components. Thus, if we assume 8-connectivity for the foreground and 4-connectivity for the background, this problem does not arise.

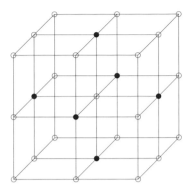

Figure 2.10: Foreground and background connectivities in 3D

In fact, it has been shown [6] that the discrete version of the Jordan theorem in 2D holds if we either use (8,4)- or (4,8)-connectivity. We will mostly assume 8-connectivity for the foreground and 4-connectivity for the background.

The same problem arises for three-dimensional images. Figure 2.10 shows an 18-connected foreground component enclosing a single background voxel which is however 18-connected to the rest of the background. The interior background voxel is not 6-adjacent to the exterior background. The continuous version of Jordan's theorem states that a simple closed surface separates two components. And again, the discrete version of this theorem is not true for all types of connectivity. It is true however for (6,26)-,(26,6)-,(18,6),- and (6,18)-images as was shown in [8] (see also [9],[10]).

The following definition makes the different connectivities used for foreground and background explicit.

Definition 2.7 Let L be a n-dimensional lattice, $n = 2, 3$. An *(m,k)-image* is a triplet (L, m, k), where $m, k \in \{4, 8\}$ if $n = 2$ and $m, k \in \{6, 18, 26\}$ if $n = 3$. In an (m, k)-image foreground raster elements are called *adjacent* if they are m-adjacent, and background raster elements are called *adjacent* if they are k-adjacent.

2.1.2 Cellular complexes

In the following, we will describe an alternative idea of capturing the notion of adjacency that will give us an intuitive way of circumventing

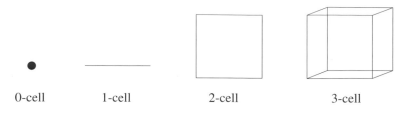

0-cell   1-cell   2-cell   3-cell

Figure 2.11: n-cells

the Jordan paradox. Although it is less often used in the literature, it is still quite useful and has received some measure of attention [11], [6].

Remember from the previous section, that digital images are matrices of grey values. In contrast, we will now define digital images as so-called *cellular complexes* which are not only composed of matrix elements but also of borders between raster elements. Thus, 3D cellular complexes contain not only cubes of voxels but also faces of voxels and points marking the vertices of voxels.

The following two definitions formalize this idea which is also illustrated in figure 2.11.

Definition 2.8 Let L be some three-dimensional discrete lattice. A *0-cell* is a lattice point, a *1-cell* is a straight line connecting two 6-adjacent 0-cells, a *2-cell* is a unit square bounded by four 1-cells, and a *3-cell* is a unit cube bounded by six adjoining 2-cells.

Definition 2.9 An *n-dimensional cellular complex* is a set C of m-cells, $m \leq n$, together with a transitive, irreflexive and antisymmetric relation $B \subset C \times C$ called a *bounding relation* such that

$$dim(c) < dim(c') \text{ for all } (c, c') \in B$$

where $dim(c)$ denotes the dimension of c, i.e. $dim(c) = m$ if c is an m-cell.

The bounding relation ensures that each cell is bounded by lower-dimensional cells. For instance, a 2-cell may be bounded by 1-cells (its faces) which in turn may be bounded by 0-cells (its vertices).

The bounding relation leads us to an alternative definition of adjacency which will naturally overcome the Jordan theorem paradox. The

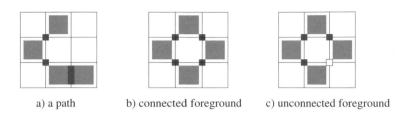

a) a path   b) connected foreground   c) unconnected foreground

Figure 2.12: Connectedness in cellular complexes

idea is to define adjacency in terms of boundedness. Two cells are said to be adjacent if one is bounding the other. Thus, a 2-cell may be adjacent to several 1-cells, but it cannot be directly adjacent to another 2-cell.

Definition 2.10 A sequence of elements $(e_0, ..., e_{k-1})$ of a cellular complex C is called a *path* if each pair of elements $(e_i, e_{i+1}), i = 0, ..., k - 2$ is adjacent, i.e. one element is bounding the other.

A subset $D \subset C$ is called *connected* iff for any two elements e, e' there exists a path from e to e'.

Figure 2.12a shows a path consisting of four 2-cells, one 1-cell and two 0-cells. Figures 2.12b,c demonstrate why the Jordan theorem poses no problem for cellular complexes. In figure 2.12b the foreground is connected as the four 2-cells are linked via four 0-cells. The background can therefore not be connected as the link between the centre pixel and the exterior background could only lead through the 0-cells which are already occupied by the foreground.

Figure 2.12c shows the reverse case. One of the 0-cells around the centre background pixel belongs to the background thus preventing the foreground path from being closed.

2.1.3   A simple border detection algorithm

In the following, we will introduce our notational conventions for describing algorithms. As a simple example, let us look at a program that will detect all border voxels in a three-dimensional binary image.

Border voxels are foreground voxels that are adjacent to at least one background voxel. If we assume 26-connectivity for the foreground and 6-connectivity for the background, border voxels are black voxels that have at least one white voxel in their 6-neighbourhood, as the following definition specifies.

Definition 2.11 A black point $p \in I$ is called a 26-border point, iff at least one of its 6-neighbours is white. It is called a 6-border point, iff at least one of its 26-neighbours is white.

Note that in the (26,6)-connectivity case we need to check the 6-neighbourhood for identifying black border points, while in the (6,26)-connectivity case, the 26-neighbourhood needs to be checked.

We will describe algorithms using the programming language C, as it is the most commonly used language for image processing. Most of the times however, we will not print entire program texts but instead only highlight the most important parts. To keep program texts short, we will usually omit variable declarations and error checking procedures whenever they are obvious.

The following variable names will be used frequently:

src	a source image
dest	a destination image
nslices	number of slices
nrows	number of rows
ncols	number of columns
slice, s, ss	slice index
row, r, rr	row index
col, c, cc	column index

We will use the term "band" interchangeably with the word "slice". Accordingly, we will often use the variables names band, b to refer to slices.

Let us now introduce some basic functions that will be used throughout this book. These functions are taken from an image processing library called *Vista* [12].

A new image is created using the function call

```
dest = VCreateImage(nbands,nrows,ncolumns);
```

This call will allocate memory space for a new raster image containing nbands number of slices of size nrows × ncolumns each and returns a pointer to this data structure which represents the output image.

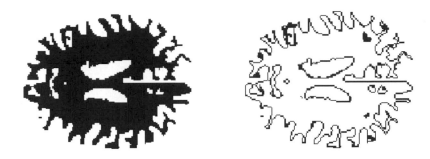

Figure 2.13: Result of the border detection algorithm

The function

```
VClearImage(dest);
```

clears an image by setting the values at all its raster locations to zero.

Referencing raster elements is accomplished by the following two functions:

```
v = VGetPixel(src,band,row,col); VSetPixel(dest,band,row,col) = v;
```

The function `VGetPixel` retrieves a grey value from the location (band,row,col) of a source image called `src`, and `VSetPixel` sets a new value at the location (band,row,col) of a destination image called `dest`.

Here now is a simple program which expects a binary image called `src` as input and returns a new binary image called `dest` as output in which only border voxels will be "black". All other voxels will be "white". Note that the algorithm does not visit voxels along the image borders so that object boundaries that meet the image borders will not be detected.

Figure 2.13 shows one slice of a three-dimensional input image which originally contained 11 slices, and the corresponding slice of the output image. Note that some parts of the object's border surface are aligned with the slice orientation so that some surface patches appear in the output image.

```
VImage VBorder3d(VImage src)
{

    dest = VCreateImage(nslices,nrows,ncols,VBitRepn);
    VClearImage(dest);

    for (slice=1; slice<nslices-1; slice++) {
        for (row=1; row<nrows-1; row++) {
            for (col=1; col<ncols-1; col++) {

                if (VGetPixel(src,slice,row,col) == 1
                    and (VGetPixel(src,slice,row,col-1) == 0
                            or VGetPixel(src,slice,row,col+1) == 0
                            or VGetPixel(src,slice,row-1,col) == 0
                            or VGetPixel(src,slice,row+1,col) == 0
                            or VGetPixel(src,slice-1,row,col) == 0
                            or VGetPixel(src,slice+1,row,col) == 0))

                    VSetPixel(dest,slice,row,col) = 1;
            }
        }
    }
    return dest;
}
```

Figure 2.14: An algorithm for detecting border voxels

2.2 Connected components

In this section, we will discuss how we can identify some simple objects in binary images. Objects that are of interest to us here are represented by *connected components* which are chunks of foreground voxels that form coherent blocks of data. In particular, we will discuss algorithms for identifying those components in binary images. Those algorithms take any binary image as input and produce as output a *labelled* image in which each foreground raster element receives a label uniquely identifying the component to which it belongs. If there are m separate components in an image there will be m such labels.

Figure 2.15 shows a two-dimensional binary image together with the corresponding labelled image. Remember from the previous section that the type of connectivity used is crucial here. For instance, if we assume 4-connectedness, there are six connected components in this image. If we assume 8-connectedness, there are just three.

1	1	0	0	0	0	0	0
1	1	1	0	0	0	0	0
1	1	1	0	0	0	0	1
0	0	1	0	0	0	0	1
0	0	0	0	0	0	1	1
0	0	0	0	0	0	1	1
0	0	0	0	0	1	1	1
0	0	1	0	0	1	1	0
0	1	0	0	0	1	1	0
1	1	1	0	0	1	1	0
0	1	0	0	1	0	0	1
0	0	0	0	1	0	0	1

1	1	0	0	0	0	0	0
1	1	1	0	0	0	0	0
1	1	1	0	0	0	0	2
0	0	1	0	0	0	0	2
0	0	0	0	0	0	2	2
0	0	0	0	0	0	2	2
0	0	0	0	0	2	2	2
0	0	3	0	0	2	2	0
0	3	0	0	0	2	2	0
3	3	3	0	0	2	2	0
0	3	0	0	2	0	0	2
0	0	0	0	2	0	0	2

Figure 2.15: A binary image and its component labelled image

2.2.1   Elementary algorithms for component labelling

A number of algorithms for identifying connected components exist both for the 2D and the 3D case, for instance [13], [14], [15], [16], [17].

Each of these algorithms has its merits and pitfalls. Some are very fast but require a lot of memory space. Others require very little memory space but are quite slow. We will begin by presenting a very simple algorithm which is relatively fast, easy to implement and usable in most situations. It is the algorithm one should always start out with. If you find that it does not satisfy your needs you should then proceed to one of the more complicated algorithms.

The basic idea underlying this algorithm is the following. We begin by selecting some arbitrary foreground voxel and assign the label "1" to it. We then explore its neighbourhood to see if there are any other foreground voxels adjacent to it. If there are, they all receive the same label as the previous voxel. We then explore the neighbourhoods of each of these new voxels in turn while propagating the label to all their neighbours until the entire conglomerate of connected voxels has received this same label. This procedure is recursively applied until no more adjacent voxels are found.

We then try to find voxels that have not received a label yet because they are not adjacent to any of the voxels we have visited so far. As soon as we have found such a voxel, we use it as a starting point for another round of labelling, this time using another label, say "2". This entire procedure is applied until all voxels have been labelled.

Note that the voxel grid can be thought of as a bi-directional graph

Figure 2.16: Voxel grid as a graph

where the nodes correspond to the voxels and adjacency relations between voxels correspond to edges (see figure 2.16). We can therefore
use well known graph search algorithms such as "depth first search" or
"breadth first search". In the following, we will discuss an implementation of such a graph search procedure for component labelling.

To conduct a depth first search, we form a stack which initially
contains only one node. Remember that a stack is a data structure from
which elements are retrieved in a "last-in-first-out" fashion, i.e. that
last element that got "pushed onto" the stack will be the first element
that will be "popped off" the stack (for more information about stacks
see for instance [18]). In our case, the first node to be pushed onto
that stack is some arbitrary foreground voxel. We then perform the
following steps until the stack becomes empty:

- Pop the next node off the stack;

- Assign the current label to it;

- Push all adjacent foreground voxels which are not yet labelled
  onto the stack.

Now search for any as yet unlabelled voxels. If one is found, increment the current label, clear the stack, push this voxel onto the stack
and perform the above procedure once again.

A breadth first search strategy is very similar to depth first search.
The only difference is that instead of using a stack which implements
a "last-in-first-out" strategy, we now use a queue, which implements a
"first-in-first-out" schedule.

This algorithm is quite easy to implement and provides a workable
solution in many cases. However, its major drawback is of course that
the stack (or the queue) may become quite large. In fact, the stack may
grow almost as large as the number of black voxels. If the foreground

occupies a large portion of the image this approach may then become infeasible. A C-style version of this algorithm is shown in figure 2.17.

2.2.2 Better algorithms for component labelling

More sophisticated labelling algorithms avoid the need to keep a stack or queue data structure which may require too much memory if the input image is large. Also, the tedious process of searching for adjacent black voxels can be avoided.

Most algorithms work in several phases, each phase involving a pass through the whole image. Some algorithms use as many as four complete passes [13], while others need only two passes [14], [16], [17]. Let us concentrate on Samet's algorithm [17], which is a very general component labelling algorithm not restricted to three-dimensional raster images. We will present a rough outline of this algorithm in a version adapted to our context of volumetric images. For a more detailed description see [17].

The algorithm is a two-pass algorithm that uses one forward pass starting at the top left corner of the first slice and a backward pass starting at the bottom right corner of the last slice. Let us now discuss the first pass.

The general idea is the following. The input image is scanned in a slice by slice fashion in which each slice is processed row by row. Each time a black voxel is encountered we check whether it is adjacent to an already labelled voxel in its immediate neighbourhood. If so, it receives the same label as its neighbour. If not, a new label is generated and attached to this voxel. Unfortunately however, connectedness cannot be determined locally as the following example shows

```
     0 1 0 1 0              0 1 0 2 0
     0 1 0 1 0              0 1 0 2 0
     0 1 1 1 0              0 1 x 2 0
     input image      initial stages of labelling
```

The fact that all black voxels in this image are 6-connected becomes evident only while inspecting the third row. At that point labels have already been attached to voxels in the first two rows. Thus, we need to record the fact that labels in the first two rows are actually equivalent, even though they initially appeared separate.

```
VImage VLabelImage3d(VImage src) // depth first connected component labelling;
{
  typedef struct {    // define a new data type for storing voxel addresses
    short b;           // band index
    short r;           // row index
    short c;           // column index
  } Voxel;
  Voxel voxel,adjacent;

  dest = VCreateImage(nbands,nrows,ncolumns); // create an output image
  initialize(dest);                           // set all voxels to zero
  label = 0;
  for (b=0; b<nbands; b++) {                   // scan the entire image
    for (r=0; r<nrows; r++) {
      for (c=0; c<ncolumns; c++) {
        if (VGetPixel(src,b,r,c) == 0) continue; // ignore background voxels
        if (VGetPixel(dest,b,r,c) > 0) continue; // already visited
        clear(&stack);                           // clear the stack for a
        label++;                                 // new component
        voxel.b = b;
        voxel.r = r;
        voxel.c = c;
        push(&stack,voxel);                      // push first node onto stack
        VSetPixel(dest,b,r,c) = label;           // and label it
        while (! empty(&stack)) {                // now do a recursive search
          pop(&stack,&voxel);                    // pop next node off the stack
                                                 // and scan its neighbourhood
          for (bb=MAX(b-1,0); bb<=MIN(b+1,nbands-1); bb++) {
            for (rr=MAX(r-1,0); rr<==MIN(r+1,nrows-1); rr++) {
              for (cc=MAX(c-1,0); cc<==MIN(c+1,ncolumns-1); cc++) {
                if (bb == voxel.b && rr == voxel.r && cc == voxel.c) continue;
                if (VGetPixel(src,bb,rr,cc) == 0) continue;
                if (VGetPixel(dest,bb,rr,cc) > 0) continue;
                adjacent.b = bb;
                adjacent.r = rr;
                adjacent.c = cc;
                push(&stack,adjacent);            // push new node onto stack
                VSetPixel(dest,bb,rr,cc) = label; // and label it
              }
            }
          }
        }
      }
    }
  }
  return dest;                                  // return the output image
}
```

Figure 2.17: Connected component labelling using depth first search

Let us use a special data structure for recording such equivalence relations between labels. The data type we need is a tree structure with the smallest label at its root, and with larger labels which are equivalent to the root label branching off.

As the labelling process moves along, new equivalences between labels may become apparent, so that the trees representing the equivalence classes involved must be merged. When several equivalence classes are merged, the class having the smallest label becomes the root of all other equivalent trees to ensure that we do not produce excessively large labels.

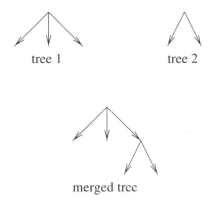

tree 1   tree 2

merged tree

After the entire image has been processed in this way, each voxel will be associated with a tree representing equivalent labels. This completes the first pass through the image.

Once every voxel has received an equivalence tree of labels, we need to resolve those equivalences to find the actual labels. This step is performed in a second pass through the entire image, which is performed in reverse order, i.e. we start at the lower right corner of the last slice and proceed to the top left corner of the first slice. After this second pass, each voxel is labelled with a unique label corresponding to the connected component it belongs to. Labels are generated in ascending order so that the largest label is equal to the number of connected components found.

track 1   track 2

Figure 2.18: Tracks

2.3   Data structures

In the previous sections we investigated binary raster images which
were represented by n-dimensional image matrices. We will now discuss
alternative ways of representing images. There are two primary reasons
why this is of importance. First of all, we would like to store binary
images in a more condensed way so that less storage space is required.
Secondly and perhaps more importantly we would like to be able to
address components found in an image in a direct way. Using image
matrices to represent an image we would have to scan the entire image
if we want to reference a particular component, which can be quite
tedious and time-consuming. In many instances, it would be preferable
if connected components or other subsets of the image matrix could be
referenced directly.

In the following, we will discuss data structures for representing
binary images as well as subsets of foreground voxels such that the
requirements listed above are met.

2.3.1   The track representation

In this section we will introduce a data structure for representing n-
dimensional binary images and subsets of images.

First let us deal with the much simpler 2D case. Two-dimensional
binary objects are often represented in a *run-length code*. The basic
idea underlying the run-length code is the following (see figure 2.18):
for each row in the binary image, record the column at which the first
non-zero pixel occurs plus the number of consecutive non-zero pixels
following that initial non-zero pixel. We call such a strip of non-zero
entries a *track*. After having found the first such track in the current
row, search for all subsequent tracks in the same row. Repeat this
process for all rows in the image.

A track in a 2D binary image can be expressed by the following data
structure:

```
{
 int     column;         // column at which non-zero entries start
 int     length;         // length (number of pixels) in the track
 pointer *next;          // pointer to the next track
}
```

The data structure for the entire 2D image is a sequence of such tracks:

```
{
 pointer row[NROWS];     // list of pointers to the tracks of each row
}
```

If we want to represent various subsets of foreground voxels separately, we use a separate sequence of tracks for each subset and store them in a list.

A straightforward generalization of this idea to the 3D case was suggested by Montani et al. [19]. They use lists of tracks for each row in each slice. We then need $n = n_r \times n_s$ lists, where n_r is the number of rows and n_s is the number of slices.

While this approach is quite easy to implement and also very efficient, it has the disadvantage of requiring a lot of memory, especially if we want to represent more than one subset within one image. We would then need an array of $n_r \times n_s$ pointers for each subset, even if it contains only a few foreground voxels.

To overcome this problem, we will use a slightly different version of 3D run-length encoding. The basic idea is to use *hash tables* instead of arrays to store the pointers to the linked lists. Hash tables are a widely used data structure that allow a quasi-direct access to pieces of data, while keeping memory requirements low. In the following, we will give a brief review of hash tables. For a more detailed reference see for instance [18, p. 360 ff.].

A hash table is an array of linked lists called *buckets*. A new element is inserted into a hash table by first selecting a bucket and appending the element to end of the bucket. The selection process is performed using a so-called *hash function* whose task it is to distribute elements evenly between available buckets such that all buckets receive roughly the same number of elements.

In our context, we can use hash tables to access tracks of consecutive non-zero voxels. A hash function that is useful for our purpose is the following:

$$hash(slice, row) = (n_s \times slice + row) \bmod H.$$

where n_s is again the number of slices in the image, and H is the maximal length of the hash table. For example, to access a track t that starts at location $slice = 8, row = 3, column = 12$, within an image containing 10 slices and a hashtable length of 100, we first compute its hash value, which is

$$hash(8, 12) = 10 \times 8 + 3 = 83.$$

Thus, track t must be somewhere inside the eighty-third bucket. To locate the track exactly, we now need to move along the linked list contained in bucket 83 until we reach the desired track. The access is fast if the linked list in that bucket is short, and it is slow if the linked list is long. Ideally, we would like the list to contain just one track. The problem then of course is that we need quite a lot of buckets to store our data. If indeed we do have sufficient storage to do just that, then our hash table implementation is exactly the same as the Sticks representation mentioned earlier.

In many cases, we do not have that much memory available and we therefore have buckets that contain more than one track.

The complete data structure written in C-style:

```
typedef struct {
  short    slice;          // slice
  short    row;            // row
  short    column;         // column at which track begins
  short    length;         // length of track
  Pointer *next;           // pointer to next track
  Pointer *previous;       // pointer to previous track
} *Track;
```

The tracks are stored in a doubly linked list, in which not only a pointer to the next track is stored but also a pointer to the previous track. Appending a track to the end of a list is much faster if we can access the end of the list directly without having to cycle through the entire list.

A *bucket* is simply a pointer to the first and to the last element of the list of tracks.

```
typedef struct {
  Pointer *first;          // pointer to first track in bucket
  Pointer *last;           // pointer to last track in bucket
} *Bucket;
```

A *volume* consists of the hash table, which is an array of buckets. Since we usually have more than one object in an image that we want to store as a volume, we store all volumes as a linked list of volumes. Hence, we need a pointer to the next volume.

```
typedef struct {
    short   label;          // volume label
    short   length;         // length of hash table (number of buckets)
    Bucket  bucket[H];      // pointers to buckets
    Pointer *next;          // pointer to next volume
} *Volume;
```

And finally, here is the data structure that allows access to all volumes in the image.

```
typedef struct {
    short nvolumes;         // number of volumes in linked list
    Pointer *first;         // pointer to first volume in linked list
    short nslices;          // number of slices in image
    short nrows;            // number of rows in image
    short ncolumns;         // number of columns
} VolumesList;
```

Converting from raster to track

Converting a binary 3D raster image to the tracks representation scheme is a straightforward process. We simply loop through all slices and rows, where in each row we seek tracks of consecutive non-zero voxels. Whenever a track is found, say in slice s, row r beginning at column c, we first compute the length of the track by moving forward within the current row until we hit the first zero voxel. As soon as we know the length of the track, we can add the track to the current volume.

Adding a track to a volume is again quite simple. We only need to establish its proper bucket within the hash table by evaluating its hash function. We then append the track to the linked list of other tracks already in that bucket. Adding a track to a bucket gets a little more complicated if we wish to keep the bucket sorted by some sorting criterion. As we shall see later on, there are good reasons for keeping buckets sorted, even at the expense of using more time to find their proper place within the linked list.

A sorting criterion might for instance be the voxel's address, where the address (s_1, r_1, c_1) is "smaller" than address (s_2, r_2, c_2) iff

$$s_1 n_s + r_1 n_r + c_1 \leq s_2 n_s + r_2 n_r + c_2,$$

where n_s are the number of slices, and n_r are the number of rows. We will come back to that later on. Here is a C-style code fragment for converting raster images to tracks.

```
for (s=0; s<nslices; s++) {
  for (r=0; r<nrows; r++) {
    c = 0;
      while (c < ncols) {
        if (VGetPixel(input_image,s,r,c) > 0) {
          track->slice  = s;
          track->row    = r;
          track->column = c;
          while (c < ncols && Voxel(input_image,s,r,c) > 0) {
            c = c + 1;
          }
          track->length = c - track->col;
          AddTrack(volume,track);
        }
        c = c + 1;
      }
  }
}
```

Converting track encoded images to raster images is even simpler. All we need to do is loop through all buckets in each volume, and replace all tracks by strings of 1s in the raster image.

2.3.2   Operations on tracks

Set Operations

The union of images is a fundamental operation used in many contexts. The union of two 3D binary images I_1 and I_2 is defined as follows:

$$(I_1 \cup I_2)(b, r, c) \ = \ I_1(b, r, c) \vee I_2(b, r, c).$$

This concept is illustrated below:

I_1 I_2 $I_1 \cup I_2$

Building unions of images in tracks representation is done in two stages: in the first stage, tracks from both input images are combined into one track represented image, in which tracks from both images may overlap. Tracks in the combined image are sorted by their addresses, so that address (b_1, r_1, c_1) is "smaller" than (b_2, r_2, c_2), iff

$$b_1 n_b + r_1 n_r + c_1 \leq s_2 n_s + r_2 n_r + c_2,$$

where n_b are the number of slices, and n_r are the number of rows. Sorting will considerably speed up the process, as we shall see in a moment. First let us go back to the merging process, i.e. the process of combining the tracks from the two volumes into one combined and sorted volume. Let `volume1` and `volume2` be the two volumes to be combined. Suppose that `volume2` is the larger of the two, i.e. the one that contains more tracks. Then the merging is performed by successively inserting tracks from `volume1` into the buckets belonging to `volume2`, using the insertion routing `AddTrack` that hashes to the correct bucket and inserts a track into its proper place within its bucket while keeping the bucket sorted by track addresses (see also [18, pp. 75ff.]). Below you see a C-code fragment for merging volumes.

```
Volume
VolumeMerge(volume1,volume2)
{
  volume0 = CopyVolume(volume2);
  for (i=0; i<volume1->length; i++) {
    for (track = volume1->bucket[i].first; track; track = track->next) {
      AddTrack(volume0,track);
    }
  }
  return volume0;
}
```

After having merged the two volumes, we must now take care of overlapping tracks. In particular, we must remove tracks completely contained in another track, or replace two or more overlapping tracks by one longer track that covers all of the overlapping tracks. The core of the algorithm cycles through the linked list in each bucket and gathers up overlapping tracks and inserts them into the corresponding output bucket.

```
Volume VolumeUnion(volume1, volume2)
{
  volume0 = VolumeMerge(volume1,volume2);
  output_volume = VolumeCreate();

  for (i=0; i< volume0->len; i++) {
    t = volume0->bucket[i].first;
    while (t != NULL) {
      r = malloc(sizeof(VTrack));
      r->band = t->band;
      r->row = t->row;
      r->col = t->col;
      s = t->next;
      u = NULL;
      ce = t->col + t->length;
      while(overlap(s,t)) {
        ce = IMAX(ce,s->col + s->length);
        u = s;
        s = s->next;
      }
      ce = t->col + t->length;
      r->length = ce - t->col;
      AddTrack(output_volume,r);
      t = s;
    }
  }
  return output_volume;
```

Note how the fact that the tracks are sorted was exploited in the
algorithm. Since the tracks are sorted, we can process the tracks in
each bucket sequentially, rather than searching through the whole list
to locate overlapping tracks.

The intersection of two volumes is defined as

$$(I_1 \cap I_2)(b,r,c) \;=\; I_1(b,r,c) \wedge I_2(b,r,c).$$

Here is a small example:

$$I_1 \qquad\qquad I_2 \qquad\qquad I_1 \cap I_2$$

Intersecting two volumes represented by tracks works essentially in
the same manner as the union building process. We begin by merging
the two volumes into one. To obtain the intersection, we then locate
overlapping tracks by looping through each bucket sequentially. Sec-

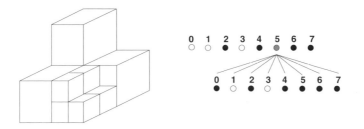

Figure 2.19: Octree construction

tions where tracks overlap are transformed into new tracks which are inserted into the output volume.

2.3.3 The octree representation

In this section, we will investigate another data representation for three-dimensional binary images called *octree encoding* [20],[21],[22]. The corresponding two-dimensional version is called a *quadtree encoding*. In the following, we will focus on the three-dimensional octree representation.

Octrees form a hierarchical subdivision of the voxel space. The voxel space in which octrees reside must have equal dimensions in all three spatial directions, and the dimensions must be a power of two. For instance, a space of size $32 \times 32 \times 32 = 2^5 \times 2^5 \times 2^5$ is legal in octree representation, whereas a space of size $32 \times 32 \times 16 = 2^5 \times 2^5 \times 2^1$ is not. The octree representation of the foreground voxels is obtained by recursively subdividing this space into octants until all voxels within each octant have a uniform value. For instance, assume we have a voxel space of dimension $4 \times 4 \times 4$, representing some object as shown in figure 2.19.

We begin by subdividing the voxel space into eight octants of size $2 \times 2 \times 2$ and inspect each octant in turn. Whenever we encounter an octant that belongs either entirely to the background ("white") or entirely to the foreground ("black"), we record that fact in our resultant octree structure. Octants that are not uniform are marked "grey" and are further subdivided into eight child nodes. In the above example, seven of the eight initial octants are uniform, and are recorded as leaves in the octree structure. The eighth octant in the lower right front part of the image requires further subdivision. The subdivision process continues until all octants are uniform.

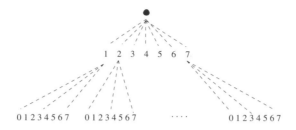

Figure 2.20: An octree

Spatial indexing

The octants produced by the process of recursive subdivision must now be indexed in some fashion so that they can be easily referenced later on. First note that we only need to reference "black" octants, as we can deduce which octants are white if we know which ones are black. In addition, it suffices to store the leaf nodes of an octree together with some information of the depth of that leaf. Thus, we only need to store a list of black octree leaves, preferably in some order that is useful for later processing.

An ordering which is widely used in this context is the so-called *"Morton sequencing"*. It was originally invented by Morton [23] for indexing maps in the Canada Geographic Information System [21]. Let us now describe how it works.

In Morton sequencing, the octants are numbered from 0 to 7 as shown in figure 2.21. Note that any voxel can be indexed by the sequence of octants in which it is contained. For example, suppose you want to index the voxel at the raster address $(5,3,7)$ which is contained in an image of size $8 \times 8 \times 8$. In the first subdivision step, this voxel is contained in octant 5, in the next it is contained in 1, and in the third subdivision it belongs to octant 3. Thus, the sequence $(5,1,3)$ gives a complete description of the voxel's position.

In order to store the entire tree, we need to store all leaf nodes. Leaf nodes that correspond to single voxels can be represented as described above. Leaf nodes that constitute blocks of voxels are encoded by the sequence of octants in which they are contained. The remaining digits are filled up by some arbitrary letter, say "X". Thus, some octant may be encoded as $(5,6,X)$. The entire octree can now be encoded as a list of leaf nodes, where each is represented by an n-tuple of digits from 0

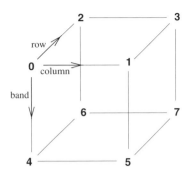

Figure 2.21: Morton codes

to 7 and the letter 'X', where n is the depth of the tree.

This list can be sorted lexically in so-called *Morton order*. For instance, some tree of depth 3 may be sorted like this: $000 < 100 < 110 < 11X < 567 < 723 < 72X$.

The prime advantage of ordering leaves in Morton order is that it arranges the leaf nodes in a fashion that corresponds to a depth first search through the tree provided the numbering of the octants is done as in figure 2.21. In other words, travelling through the list of leaf nodes in Morton order corresponds to a depth first traversal of the octree as can be seen in figure 2.20. (Remember that in depth first traversal of a tree you begin by exploring the left-most branch of the tree until you reach its leaf node, and you then backtrack to the deepest node along this branch which has an as yet unexplored branch and follow this branch to its entire depth and so on).

Clearly, we must devise efficient ways of maintaining an octree. In particular, we need to delete nodes, insert nodes or look up a node. Note that our octree is really a sorted linear list of nodes. An efficient way of storing a sorted list is given by the *binary search tree method*. A binary search tree is a binary tree with the following properties (see [18, p. 258 ff.]):

- Each node has at most two child nodes, namely a "left" child and a "right" child.

- Each node has a unique label, and the set of all labels is sorted by some given criterion. In our case, the sorting is given by the Morton order.

- An in-order traversal of the tree preserves the order of the nodes. (In in-order traversal each node is visited after exploring the left subtree, but before traversing the right subtree). In other words, at each node x of the tree the following holds: all nodes in the left subtree of x have labels less than x and all nodes in the right subtree have labels greater than x.

The maintenance of a sorted list can be quite efficiently handled using this data structure. We will not go into further detail at this point. For more detail see for instance [18, p. 258 ff.].

Raster to octree conversion

Normally, images are acquired in raster format, so that we need algorithms for converting raster images into octree representations. Several such algorithms exist [22], [24]. In the following, we will present Holroyd's algorithm[25] in more detail.

The basic idea is the following: we scan the raster image voxel by voxel successively encoding blocks of foreground voxels into octree nodes. However, the order in which we scan the image is not the usual band-wise left to right scan order but the Morton order as introduced above. The advantage is that voxels belonging to the same node in the resulting octree will be listed in sequence so that merging them into larger blocks will be easy.

Clearly, we need a function for decoding Morton addresses, which converts a given Morton code into a raster address given as a band, row, column)-triplet. This is really quite easy. We process each character of the Morton code in turn. Note that the position within the sequence encodes the depth level of the tree which translates into an offset of the resulting address. The exact algorithm is given below.

```
void
DecodeMorton(unsigned char *code,int *band,int *row,int *column,
    int *level, int n)
{
    int i,power;
    unsigned char c;

    (*level)= 0;
    (*band)= 0;
    (*row)= 0;
    (*column)= 0;
```

```
power = 1;
for (i=1; i<n; i++) power *= 2;

for (i=0; i<n; i++) {
   c = *(code+i);
   if (c==X) {
      c = 0;
      (*level)++;
   }

   (*band) += (c % 2) * power;
   (*row) += ((c / 2) % 2) * power;
   (*column) += (c / 4) * power;
   power /= 2;
   }
}
```

The raster to octree conversion now proceeds as follows: we generate a complete sequence of Morton codes sorted in Morton order so that every Morton code appears in this sequence. Each Morton code is then converted into its raster address using the function DecodeMorton. This allows us to loop through each voxel in Morton order assembling consecutive foreground voxels into octants as we go along.

Octree to raster conversion

Converting an image from octree representation back into raster representation is much easier. All we have to do is to successively process each node in the octree by first determining its depth within the tree which determines the size of the block it represents, finding the voxel coordinates of its top left corner by converting Morton code into a raster address again using the function MortonDecode and then setting all voxels in this block to "1".

Note that we have used the function MortonDecode for both raster to octree conversion as well as for the reverse octree to raster conversion. For the sake of completeness let us now briefly discuss Morton encoding, which converts a raster address into a Morton code.

The basic idea is to loop through an index representing the depth of the tree where at each depth level the (band, row, column)-address is converted to a corresponding octant identification number. When all depth levels have been processed a Morton sequence will have been generated (see C-code on next page).

```
void MortonEncode (int band, int row, int column,int level, int n,
                   unsigned char **code)
{
   int power, i;
   unsigned char *c,X=8;

   c = calloc (n,sizeof (unsigned char));
   *code = c;

   power = 1;
   for (i=1; i<n; i++) power *= 2;

   for (i=n-1; i>=level; i--) {
      *c = 0;
      if (band >= power) {
         *c = 1;
         band -= power;
      }
      if (row >= power) {
         *c += 2;
         row -= power;
      }
      if (column >= power) {
         *c += 4;
         column -= power;
      }
      c++;
      power /= 2;
   }
   for (i=level; i>=0; i--)
      *(c++)=X;
}
```

2.3.4   Operations on octrees

Let us now discuss some basic operations on octrees.

One of the most basic operations is to check whether a voxel at a given raster address is a foreground voxel. This checking operation requires two steps: we first have to encode the raster address into Morton code using EncodeMorton and then search the linear octree for the presence of this code. If the linear octree is represented as a binary search tree, this lookup operation will take $O(\log n)$ steps where n is the number of foreground voxels.

Another basic operation is zooming in (scaling up) by a factor of two or any power of two. This operation is quite easily performed using octrees. All there is to do is to remove the root node of the octree and replace it by one of its child nodes. Similarly, zooming out (or scaling down) by a factor of two can be performed by adding an additional root

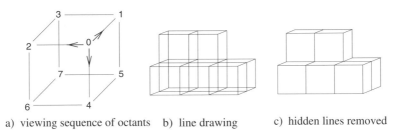

a) viewing sequence of octants   b) line drawing   c) hidden lines removed

Figure 2.22: Visualizations using octrees

node.

One of the reasons for the great popularity of octrees are their use-fulness for 3D visualization routines. Suppose you want to visualize a three-dimensional voxel image from a given viewpoint, for instance the set of voxels shown in figure 2.22b,c. Clearly, in displaying such an image, hidden lines, which are not visible from the current viewpoint, must be removed. Octrees provide a very easy mechanism for avoiding the display of hidden lines, as a spatial ordering is already entailed in Morton sequencing.

For instance, to visualize the octants shown in figure 2.22a from a top right viewpoint we can simply list the octants lexically as (0, 1, 2, 3, 4, 5, 6, 7) to obtain a sequence of octants such that no octant can be visually blocked by any following octant. Specifically, octant 0 can not be blocked by any octant 1 to 7, octant 1 cannot be blocked by octants 2 to 7, and so on. Thus, a natural order in which octants must be projected onto the viewing plane is given. Clearly, some other sequences of octants would also work in this case, for instance (0, 6, 4, 2, 1, 5, 3, 7). Likewise, for any other viewing direction there will be some ordering of octants that is spatially appropriate.

Note that because of the hierarchical structure of octrees any octants contained in an octant can also not be blocked by any subsequent octant in this sequence. Thus, the octree encoding provides a very efficient way of visualizing voxel volumes. In fact, voxel volumes are frequently converted into octree representation solely for rendering purposes.

We will not go into more detail at this point. Further information about operations on octrees can be found for instance in [22], [15], [26].

Chapter 3

Features of 3D components

3.1 Topological characteristics of 3D objects

Sometimes it is useful to derive shape descriptions of binary objects that are invariant under certain flexible transformations. Imagine an elastic object that is stretched, twisted or bent without tearing cracks or holes into its surface, and without allowing some parts of the surface to touch other parts of the surface. Such transformations will inevitably change many properties of the object, in particular the object's size, its curvature or its orientation in space. However, there are some parameters that will remain unchanged. For instance, the number of connected components will not be changed. There are two more parameters that also remain unchanged, one is called the *Euler Number*, the other one is called the *Genus*. In the following, we will discuss these parameters in more detail.

3.1.1 Components, cavities and handles

Let us begin by discussing the *Euler Number*. Intuitively speaking, the Euler number is a combination of several topological characteristics. It combines the number of connected components, the number of "cavities" and the number of "handles" protruding from the object. Let us look at each of these parameters in turn.

Connected components have been discussed at length in the previous chapter. So we need not go into more detail here.

Let us now look at cavities. A cavity is a totally enclosed compo-

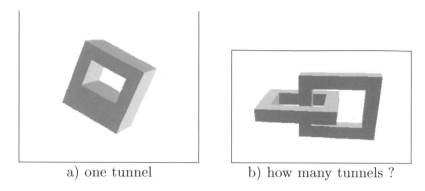

a) one tunnel   b) how many tunnels ?

Figure 3.1: Counting the number of tunnels

nent of the background. It is easy to count the number of cavities using the algorithms for computing the number of connected components introduced in section 2.2. All we have to do is to invert the image so that all black voxels become white and vice versa. We then compute the connected components of the background and subtract the component that surrounds the foreground.

A much more difficult concept to grasp is the "handles". A handle has sometimes been identified with the concept of a "tunnel", i.e. a hole that has two exits to the surface. Figure 3.1a shows an object that clearly has one tunnel, and no cavity. But what about figure 3.1b? It is not at all easy to count "handles" much less "tunnels" in that object. A more stringent definition that will help us clarify what we mean by a "handle" is the so-called *first Betti-Number* [27]. The first Betti-Number counts the maximum number of non-separating cuts one can make through the object without producing more connected components, where a "cut" must fully penetrate the object (the "knife" must not be "withdrawn"). Figure 3.2 shows examples of such cuts. There are any number of separating and non-separating cuts conceivable for this object. But once you have decided on one particular non-separating cut there are no further non-separating cuts possible since any further cut would slice the object in two. Thus, the Betti-Number for this object is one.

Similarly, we can now compute the Betti-Number for the mysterious object in figure 3.1b. Clearly, there are two non-separating cuts possible for this object, one for each component.

Sometimes, the first Betti-Number is also called the *genus* of the

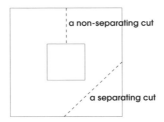

Figure 3.2: Separating and non-separating cuts

object. In the following, we will use the terms "first Betti-Number", "genus", "number of handles" and "number of tunnels" synonymously.

3.1.2 Computing the Euler number

So far we have introduced three parameters – the number of connected components, cavities and the genus. We are now ready to define the *Euler number* which combines all three entities.

The Euler number is defined as the number of connected components plus the number of cavities minus the genus [28]:

$$euler \; = \; \#components \; + \; \#cavities \; - \; genus. \qquad (3.1)$$

The Euler number is clearly a global feature of an object. Global features seem to call for algorithms that are also global in the sense that they search through the entire image at each step of the procedure. Global computations are undesirable as they are extremely tedious and time-consuming to compute.

As we have seen in the previous chapter, the number of connected components cannot be computed locally, as we either need to perform a global graph search or keep some global equivalence table. This seems to suggest that the Euler number cannot be computed locally either. Surprisingly however, this is not the case. It is in fact possible to compute both the Euler number and the genus by purely local computations, i.e. by investigating small neighbourhoods. To understand why, we will need some mathematical background. Our presentation here follows [27], [28], [29], and [30].

It is a well known fact that the genus of a digital object can be computed by investigating the surfaces that enclose the object and its cavities. If the object is digital, the enclosing surfaces consist of a fabric

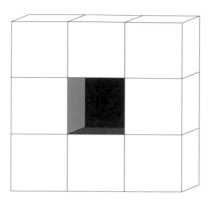

Figure 3.3: An object with one tunnel

of polyhedra. Such surfaces are called *netted surfaces*. They are made up of vertices, edges and faces of voxels. It has been shown[31] that the genus of a netted surface can be computed by counting the number of its vertices, edges and faces. More precisely,

$$2 - 2\,genus = \#vertices - \#edges + \#faces. \qquad (3.2)$$

Using this fact, we can indeed compute the genus by local operations. For instance, the genus of the surface enclosing the object shown in figure 3.3 can be computed as follows.

$$\#faces = 32$$
$$\#edges = 64$$
$$\#vertices - 32$$

And so
$$2 - 2\,genus = 32 - 64 + 32 = 0.$$

Sometimes, it may happen that two closed netted surfaces meet at a single edge. Such edges are counted twice – once for each surface they belong to.

Let us now look at the Euler number which can be computed from the number of connected components, the cavities and the genus. Each connected component and cavity is wrapped up in a netted surface

S_i. If there are K number of connected components and C number of cavities, the number of such surfaces will be $K + C$. The genus of each surface can be computed using equation 3.2 Note that each of these closed surfaces encloses a single connected component or a single cavity so that by 3.1

$$euler_i \ = \ 1 \ - \ genus_i$$

and thus

$$2 \ - \ 2 \, genus_i \ = \ 2 \ - \ 2 \, (1 \ - \ euler_i) \ = \ 2 \, euler_i,$$

where $euler_i$ denotes the Euler number of a single connected component. Therefore,

$$2 \, euler \ = \ \sum_{i=1}^{K+C} 2 \, euler_i \qquad (3.3)$$

$$= \ \sum_{i=1}^{K+C} (2 - 2genus_i) \qquad (3.4)$$

$$= \ \sum_{i=1}^{K+C} \#vertices_i \ - \ \#edges_i \ + \ \#faces_i \qquad (3.5)$$

In other words, we can compute the Euler number of a digital object by counting vertices, edges and faces.

Counting edges and vertices is not as easy as it seems. It does not suffice to identify all surface voxels and add their vertices, edges and faces, as many edges and surfaces would be counted twice that way. Many solutions to this problem have been suggested [32], [33], [34]. An alternative method is described in [29], [30] based on a slightly different line of reasoning. The algorithm is reported below in a C-style version. For a complete proof of its correctness see [29], [30].

The algorithm computes the Euler number of a 3D digital object which is assumed to be 6-connected. The foreground voxels must not touch the image boundaries. This can always be achieved by placing an additional layer of background voxels around the image boundaries in all directions.

To compute the Euler number of a 26-connected object, we can exploit the following duality formula:

$$euler_6(S) \;=\; euler_{26}(\bar{S})$$
$$euler_{26}(S) \;=\; euler_6(\bar{S})$$

where S denotes the image foreground and $\bar{S}$ its background and $euler_k$, $k = 6, 26$ denotes the Euler number of a k-connected object. We can therefore compute the Euler number of a 26-connected image foreground by computing the Euler number of its 6-connected background. In figure 3.4 the C-program text is listed.

3.2   Simple shape features

A ubiquitous problem in image processing is the identification or classification of structures found in digital images. The structures to be identified may for instance be connected components or some sets of connected components. In order to identify such objects, we need to find suitable features that can be used to characterize them. In the following, we will discuss some simple features that are sometimes useful in describing properties of objects.

3.2.1   Size

The feature that is most easily computed for any binary object is its size. All we have to do is to sum up the number of foreground voxels. The only point of interest in discussing the computation of an object's size is the computational efficiency of the algorithm used. As we shall see, the time needed to compute this feature depends primarily on the type of representation that we use to encode the image and its objects.

Suppose the image is coded in raster format and the objects are represented as labels where each object is encoded by a unique label. We now want to compute the size of the object encoded by some specific label, say "42". We then have to loop through all voxels of the entire image counting all voxels that have label "42". Clearly, this is a somewhat slow procedure. It would be much more advantageous to use a representation in which we would not have to inspect every single voxel along the way. Both octrees and track representations can be helpful here.

```
neuler = 0;
for (b=1; b<nbands-1; b++) {
  for (r=1; r<nrows-1; r++) {
    for (c=1; c<ncolumns-1; c++) {

      if (VGetPixel(image, b, r, c) == 0) continue;

      x1 = VGetPixel(image, b,   r+1, c);
      x2 = VGetPixel(image, b,   r,   c+1);
      x3 = VGetPixel(image, b+1, r,   c);
      x4 = VGetPixel(image, b,   r+1, c+1);
      x5 = VGetPixel(image, b+1, r+1, c);
      x6 = VGetPixel(image, b+1, r,   c+1);
      x7 = VGetPixel(image, b+1, r+1, c+1);

      nx1 = NOT(x1);  // negated versions: nx1 = (x1 > 0)? 0 : 1
      nx2 = NOT(x2);
      nx3 - NOT(x3);
      nx4 = NOT(x4);
      nx5 = NOT(x5);
      nx6 = NOT(x6);

      if (nx1 * nx2 * nx3 -- 1) {
        psi = 1;
      }
      else if ((x7 == 0) || (nx4 + nx5 + nx6 > 1)) {
        psi = x1 * x2 * x3  -  x1 * x2 * nx4  -  x1 * x3 * nx5
          -  x2 * x3 * nx6;
      }
      else {
        psi = - x1 * x2 * nx3 * nx4
          -  x1 * nx2 * x3 * nx5  -  nx1 * x2 * x3 * nx6;
      }
      neuler += psi;
    }
  }
}
```

Figure 3.4: Algorithm for computing the Euler number (6-adjacency)

In track representation we only have to loop through all tracks belonging to the object and add their lengths. Depending on the average lengths of the tracks we usually obtain a considerable speed-up. Below a C-style piece of code is given.

```
{
    isize = 0;
    for (i=0; i<VolumeNBuckets(v); i++) {
        for (t = VFirstTrack(v,i); VTrackExists(t); t = VNextTrack(t))
            isize += VTrackLength(t);
    }
    return isize;
}
```

In octree representation, we process each node in Morton order by computing its size and adding up the sizes as we move from one node to the next. Recall from chapter 1 that a node's size can be deduced from its Morton code by counting the number of letters "X" in the code.

3.2.2   Shape similarity measures

A class of quite useful shape measures computes the similarity of some object to some well known object, for instance a sphere or a box. In other words, those measures determine how closely the object resembles a sphere or a box.

Let us begin with the similarity measure for the box shape. The principal idea is the following: if the object were a perfect box, then the smallest enclosing box would have the same volume as the entire object. If the object were very dissimilar from a box then its volume would be very different from that of the enclosing box.

To compute this measure, we first have to determine the volume of the smallest enclosing box. In our track representation, we simply loop through all tracks and locate the smallest and largest values for the band, row and column coordinates of all tracks. Thus, we can easily compute the size of the smallest enclosing box as:

$$size_{box} = (b_1 - b_0) * (r_1 - r_0) * (c_1 - c_0)$$

where b_1, r_1, c_1 denote the largest band-, row- and column-coordinates of the object, and b_0, r_0, c_0 denote its smallest coordinates.

The similarity measure can then be defined as

$$similarity_{box} = \frac{size_{object}}{size_{box}}.$$

Analogously, we can define a measure for the similarity to a sphere. We begin by computing the smallest enclosing sphere, whose centre coincides with the centroid of the object.

The centroid $g = (g_b, g_r, g_c)$ is defined as follows:

$$g_b = \frac{1}{size} \sum_{b,r,c} b\, f(b,r,c), \tag{3.6}$$

$$g_r = \frac{1}{size} \sum_{b,r,c} r\, f(b,r,c), \tag{3.7}$$

$$g_c = \frac{1}{size} \sum_{b,r,c} c\, f(b,r,c), \tag{3.8}$$

where $size$ denotes the number of foreground voxels and $f(b,r,c)$ is the grey value function of the image, i.e.

$$f(b,r,c) = \begin{cases} 1, & \text{if lattice point } (b,r,c) \text{ is black} \\ 0, & \text{otherwise} \end{cases}$$

We now have to compute the distance from g to all border voxels. The largest such distance determines the radius of the smallest enclosing sphere. Note that the track representation is particularly well suited to this task. The largest distance from the centroid to a border voxel can only occur at the end-points of a track. Thus, we simply loop through all tracks and compute the distance to both end-points of each track. Below is a piece of C-code.

```
{
  rmax = 0;
  for (i=0; i<VolumeNBuckets(v); i++) {  // loop through all tracks
    for (t = VFirstTrack(v,i); VTrackExists(t); t = VNextTrack(t))

      u = t->band - center[0];    // determine distance from centre
      v = t->row  - center[1];
      w = t->col  - center[2];
      d = u * u + v * v + w * w;
      if (d > rmax) rmax = d;   // find the largest distance
```

```
    w = t->col + t->length   - mean[2]; // check the second endpoint
    d = u * u + v * v + w * w;
    if (d > rmax) rmax = d;
  }
}
return sqrt(dmax);    // return the result
```

Remember from elementary geometry that the volume of a sphere of radius r is given by

$$size_{sphere} = \frac{4 * r^3 * \pi}{3},$$

so that we can easily compute the volume of the smallest enclosing sphere once its radius has been determined.

We can now define the similarity measure as follows:

$$similarity_{sphere} = \frac{size_{object}}{size_{sphere}}.$$

In a similar way, we can define the *compactness* of an object. Compactness measures the ratio of an object's surface and its volume. Clearly, a sphere is maximally compact. We can therefore measure the compactness of any arbitrary object by comparing it with the compactness of a sphere. From elementary geometry we know that for a sphere whose surface size is s and whose volume is v the following holds:

$$v = \sqrt{\frac{s^3}{\pi}}$$

Let us then define the compactness of an object as:

$$compactness = \frac{volume}{\sqrt{\pi}\ surface^{3/2}}.$$

The compactness will be 1 if the object is a sphere, and it will be larger than 1 for any other object. For digital images, the surface size of an object can be determined by computing the number of its border voxels (for instance using the algorithm described in section 2.1.3).

Certainly, many alternative shape measures may be derived using similar lines of reasoning. For more information see for instance [35], [36].

3.3 Moments

In this section, we will study another approach to characterizing the shape of objects. The type of features we will investigate are *moments*, which play an important role in statistics. The shape of a multidimensional probability distribution in statistics is often characterized by features such as its principal axes or covariance. We can use analogous measures to characterize the shape of any object in n-dimensional space.

3.3.1 Definition

Let us begin by introducing some basic terms.

Definition 3.1 The *(i,j,k)-moment* of a three-dimensional digital image is defined as follows:

$$m_{ijk} = \sum_{b,r,c} b^i r^j c^k f(b,r,c)$$

where $f(b,r,c)$ is the grey value function with

$$f(b,r,c) = \begin{cases} 1, & \text{if } (b,r,c) \text{ is a foreground voxel,} \\ 0, & \text{otherwise} \end{cases}$$

The *order of a moment* m_{ijk} is defined to be the sum $(i + j + k)$.

Moments can be used to characterize objects. In fact, if all moments of two objects exist and are identical then the two objects are the same.

In the previous section, we already encountered some moments. For instance, the size of an object can also be characterized by its (0,0,0)-moment:

$$m_{000} = \sum_{b,r,c} f(b,r,c).$$

Secondly, the centroid $g = (g_b, g_r, g_c)$ as defined by equation 3.8 is given by the following first-order moments:

$$
\begin{aligned}
g_b &= m_{100}/m_{000} \\
g_r &= m_{010}/m_{000} \\
g_c &= m_{001}/m_{000}
\end{aligned}
$$

Note that the definition of moments we have presented so far is not invariant with regard to position within the image lattice. In other words, if an object is shifted within the image lattice towards a new position its moments will change. If we want to describe an object's shape irrespective of the object's location this is clearly undesirable. The easiest way to overcome this problem is to shift objects into a standard location before computing its moments. The standard location that we choose is of course the object's centroid. The following definition captures this idea.

Definition 3.2 Let $g = (g_b, g_r, g_c)$ be the centroid of some three-dimensional digital image I. The *central (i,j,k)-moment M_{ijk}* of I is defined as:

$$M_{ijk} = \sum_{b,r,c} (b - g_b)^i (r - g_r)^j (c - g_c)^k f(b, r, c)$$

Thus, for the computation of central moments the object's centroid is shifted into the origin of the image lattice. In the following, we will mostly use central moments rather than general moments.

Orientation

A task often encountered in image processing involves finding the best match between a given object and a set of objects in some image database, where the objects to be compared might be in any arbitrary and unknown orientation. An approach frequently used to solve this problem is to first rotate all objects into a standard orientation and perhaps also scale them to a standard size before comparing them. In the following, we will discuss a method based on the use of moments to achieve this.

We will assume that an object is given as a set of black voxels in some image lattice. Let us begin by defining an object's orientation. Our goal is to define a coordinate system whose origin resides in the object's centroid and whose coordinate axes are oriented in a standardized way such as the one shown in figure 3.5. Such a coordinate system is sometimes called *object centered*.

Note that in figure 3.5 one of the coordinate axes points in the direction of the largest extent of the object, while another axis points

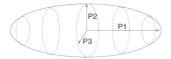

Figure 3.5: Principal axes of an object

in the direction of the smallest extent, and the third points in a direction
of intermediate extent. All three axes are mutually perpendicular.

Ellipsoids such as the one shown in figure 3.5 can be represented by
the *inertia matrix*, which is a symmetric matrix defined by the second-
order central moments as follows[37], [38]:

$$
I = \begin{bmatrix}
Ixx & -Ixy & -Ixz \\
-Iyx & Iyy & -Iyz \\
-Izx & -Izy & Izz
\end{bmatrix}
$$

where

$$
\begin{aligned}
I_{xx} &= \mu_{020} + \mu_{002} \\
I_{yy} &= \mu_{200} + \mu_{002} \\
I_{zz} &= \mu_{200} + \mu_{020}
\end{aligned}
$$

And, exploiting symmetry:

$$
\begin{aligned}
I_{xy} &= I_{yx} = \mu_{110} \\
I_{xz} &= I_{zx} = \mu_{101} \\
I_{yz} &= I_{zy} = \mu_{011}.
\end{aligned}
$$

Since the inertia matrix is symmetric its eigenvalues must be real.
If R is the matrix of its eigenvectors, and $(\lambda_0, \lambda_1, \lambda_2)$ its cigcnvalucs,
then the following holds:

$$
R^T I R = \begin{bmatrix}
\lambda_0 & 0 & 0 \\
0 & \lambda_1 & 0 \\
0 & 0 & \lambda_2
\end{bmatrix}
$$

The eigenvector corresponding to the largest eigenvalue determines
the direction of the largest dispersion of the object, the second largest

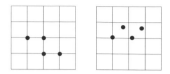

Figure 3.6: Non-discrete coordinates produced by rotation

eigenvalue corresponds to the second largest dispersion, and so forth. Thus, the eigenvectors of the inertia matrix define a coordinate system such as the one in figure 3.5. The eigenvectors of the inertia matrix are called the *principal axes* of the object.

The principal axes define an object centered coordinate system well suited to the task of doing rotationally invariant comparisons. In fact, the eigenvectors form the rows of a rotation matrix that aligns the principal axes with this new coordinate system. Thus, multiplying the object with R produces a rotated version of the object such that the principal axes coincide with the coordinate axes in this new system.

Note that rotating points in a discrete lattice by an arbitrary angle will usually not produce valid integer coordinates within this lattice (see figure 3.6). At this point we simply move round this problem by allowing points to have real coordinates. We will come back to this problem in chapter 6.

Unfortunately, the orientation of our new coordinate system is not uniquely defined, as one can easily see from the fact that

$$
\begin{aligned}
I v_i &= \lambda_i v_i \\
I(\ v_i) &= \lambda_i (-v_i)
\end{aligned}
$$

for any eigenvector v_i of I.

Thus, there are eight different orientations conceivable, corresponding to the possible combinations of $\{\pm v_0, \pm v_1, \pm v_2\}$. If we restrict the coordinate system to be right-handed, four of these are excluded, still leaving an undesirable ambiguity. Figure 3.7 shows the remaining four orientations.

Depending on the task at hand, various solutions for resolving this ambiguity can be adopted.

Galvez et al. [38] for instance suggest using the following heuristic:

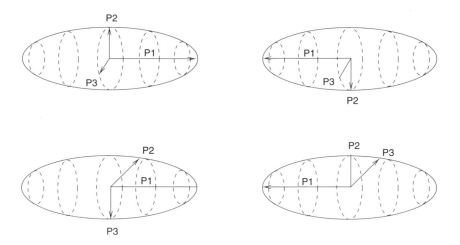

Figure 3.7: Ambiguity of orientation

- Let v_0 be the eigenvector corresponding to the largest eigenvalue. Search along the directions of v_0 and $-v_0$ for the point that is most distant from the centroid. If this point is found along the direction of v_0 use v_0, else use $-v_0$.

- Use the same procedure to identify the second largest axis.

- As the coordinate system must be right-handed and orthogonal, the third axis can be identified using the cross-product:

$$v_2 = v_0 \times v_1.$$

Let us now come back to our initial task of comparing objects by first rotating them into a standard orientation. Sometimes, the objects to be compared come not only in an arbitrarily rotated version but are also not properly scaled. Fortunately, we can use the same approach to scale objects to standard size. Remember that the eigenvalues of the inertia matrix determine the dispersion along the principal axes. We can use this information to scale objects so that some predefined dispersion along each axis is achieved.

3.3.2 Features derived from moments

The fact that the eigenvalues of the inertia matrix determine the dispersion along the principal axes can also be used to characterize important

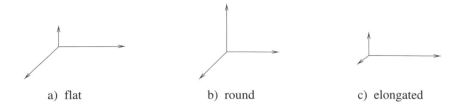

a) flat   b) round   c) elongated

Figure 3.8: Shape features derived from moments

features of an object. Let $(\lambda_0, \lambda_1, \lambda_2)$ be the three eigenvalues sorted by value so that λ_0 represents the largest value, and λ_2 the smallest.

Clearly, if λ_2 is much smaller than λ_1, the object will be flat, because its dispersion about one of its principal axes is small, and large about the other two axes. In this case, the ratio

$$\frac{\lambda_2}{\lambda_1}$$

will be large.

Similarly, the object will be sphere-shaped if the three eigenvalues are about the same, which can be tested by the ratio

$$\frac{\lambda_0}{\lambda_2}.$$

Lastly, the object will be elongated, or shaped like a stick, if the two smaller eigenvalues are about the same in size but much smaller than the largest value, so that that ratio

$$\frac{\lambda_0}{\lambda_1}$$

is large. Figure 3.8 shows these three cases.

Invariants

So far we have studied the eigenvalues of the inertia matrix as features for object recognition tasks. However, there are a number of other features that can be derived from the central moments of an object. As before, we are primarily interested in obtaining features that are invariant with respect to linear transformations such as rotation, translation or scaling.

Several approaches for obtaining such invariant features have been reported in the literature [39], [40]. As the mathematics is quite involved, we will not present the mathematical background here, but simply report some results.

Sadjadi [39], for instance, arrives at the following set of second-order moment invariants:

$$
\begin{aligned}
J_1 &= m_{200} + m_{020} + m_{002} \\
J_2 &= m_{200}m_{020} + m_{200}m_{002} + m_{020}m_{002} - m_{101}^2 - m_{110}^2 - m_{011}^2 \\
J_3 &= m_{200}m_{020}m_{002} - m_{002}m_{110}^2 + 2m_{110}m_{101}m_{011} \\
&\quad - m_{020}m_{101}^2 - m_{200}m_{011}^2.
\end{aligned}
$$

Note that these values can be computed quite efficiently. We do not need to set up the entire inertia matrix and compute its eigenvalues. In cases where computational efficiency is critical, the use of the above values might be advantageous. One of the disadvantages of these values is however that their geometrical meaning is usually quite obscure.

Lo et al. [40] arrive at another set of invariants which we will not discuss here.

Chapter 4

Operations on 3D binary images

In this chapter, we will discuss operations on three-dimensional binary images. Such operations take any three-dimensional binary image as input and produce some output image which usually has the same number of slices, rows and columns as the input image but which need not be binary.

We may for instance want to measure distances between binary objects in an image. An algorithm performing such measurements takes any binary image as input and produces an image containing distance measurements as output.

4.1 Topological classification

In this section, we will discuss an algorithm for classifying voxels according to their topological type. Topological types pertaining to voxels are for instance "surface voxel" or "curve voxel". Figure 4.1 shows the topological types identifiable in an image. The task of classifying voxels within an image according to their topological type is called *topological classification* [41], [42]. These types are summarized on the next page in table 4.1.

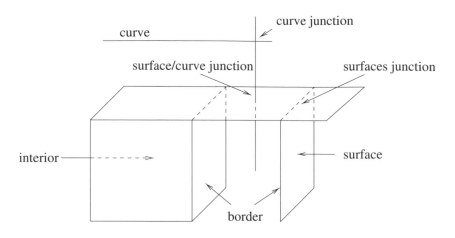

Figure 4.1: Topological types

1   interior point
2   isolated point
3   border point
4   curve point
5   curve(s) junction
6   surface point
7   surface/curve(s) junction
8   surfaces junction
9   surfaces/curve(s) junction

Table 4.1: Topological types

We will now discuss classification methods for identifying these types. Our discussion in this section follows the presentation given in [42]. Let us begin with the continuous case. Suppose we want to distinguish points on a surface from interior points of some object (see figure 4.2).

Clearly, for each point on a surface we can find some neighbourhood small enough to be cut into two pieces by the surface so that both pieces belong to different parts of the image background. Any neighbourhood smaller than this neighbourhood will have the same property, i.e. it will also be cut into two background pieces.

On the other hand, for a point which lies in the interior of some object, there will be a small neighbourhood entirely enclosed by the object. Any neighbourhood smaller than this one will also be enclosed

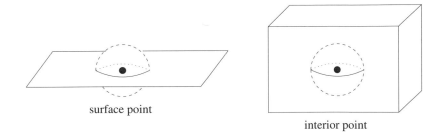

surface point

interior point

Figure 4.2: Distinguishing topological types

by the object.

Thus, the number of connected components of the image's background in a small neighbourhood around the point is an important clue to its topological type. We will call these components *background components*.

However, even though the number of background components is important it does not suffice for distinguishing between all topological types as can be seen in figure 4.3. The number of background components is 1 for interior points, curve points and curve junction points.

In order to distinguish between these types we need to consider foreground components as well. Unfortunately, the number of foreground components as such is quite inclusive, as it equals 1 in all cases. However, eliminating the point under consideration will help. Notice that deleting this point will cause the foreground to fall apart into several pieces, so that the number of such pieces becomes indicative of the topological type. Let us call connected components of the foreground with the central point eliminated *foreground components*.

More precisely, let X denote the set of points belonging to the object, and let N^* denote the set of points belonging to the small neighbourhood around the point under consideration, not including the point itself. Then the foreground components are the connected subsets of the set

$$X \cap N^*.$$

For instance, the number of foreground components around the curve junction point in figure 4.3 equals 4, whereas the number of components around the curve point equals 2.

Likewise, let $\bar{X}$ denote the points of the image not belonging to the

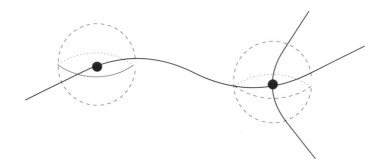

Figure 4.3: Identifying curve point and curve junctions

object, and let N denote the set of points belonging to the small neighbourhood around the point under consideration including the point itself. Then the background components are the connected subsets of the set

$$\bar{X} \cap N.$$

In order to distinguish between all types of point we need to take both the number of foreground components and the number of background components into account. Figure 4.4 shows several different types of surface junction. Note that both the surface point and the surface/curve junction have two background components. However, the surface point has just one foreground component, whereas the junction point has two foreground components, namely the part of the curve above the surface and the part below.

We have now identified a number of criteria for distinguishing between various topological types. Table 4.2 summarizes our results, where $\bar{C}$ denotes the number of background components and C^* denotes the number of foreground components.

So far we have only considered continuous images in which boundaries are smooth. We will now apply the same considerations to discrete binary raster images so as to classify voxels according to their topological type.

The main point that we need to consider is how to adapt the definitions of the background and foreground neighbourhoods that played such a vital role in the continuous case. In the following, let X be the set of foreground voxels, and $N_k(x)$ denote the k-neighbourhood of voxel x including voxel x, and let $N_k^*(x)$ denote the k-neighbourhood of voxel

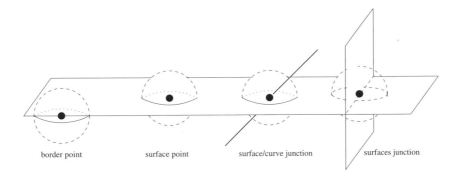

Figure 4.4: Distinguishing border points, surface points and surface/curve junctions

1	interior point	$\bar{C} = 0$	
2	isolated point		$C^* = 0$
3	border point	$\bar{C} = 1$	$C^* = 1$
4	curve point	$\bar{C} = 1$	$C^* = 2$
5	curves junction	$\bar{C} = 1$	$C^* > 2$
6	surface point	$\bar{C} = 2$	$C^* = 1$
7	surface/curve(s)-junction	$\bar{C} = 2$	$C^* \geq 2$
8	surfaces junction	$\bar{C} > 2$	$C^* = 2$
9	surfaces/curve(s)-junction	$\bar{C} > 2$	$C^* \geq 2$

Table 4.2: Topological types

x not including voxel x.

Remember from section 2.1 that we generally use 26-connectivity for the foreground and 6-connectivity for the background. Thus, a straightforward adaptation of our previous definitions of foreground and background components to the discrete case is to use the number of 26-connected foreground components within a small neighbourhood which are 26-adjacent to the voxel in question, and the number of 6-connected background components 6-adjacent to the centre.

Remember from the beginning of this section that we need to consider neighbourhoods around x which are connected and which satisfy the requirement that for any neighbourhood contained in it the number of foreground and background components does not change. To make

our definitions as stringent as possible we would clearly like to choose
the smallest such neighbourhoods.

Clearly, we must choose the 26-neighbourhood for the foreground
components. As any 26-connected component must be 26-adjacent to
x, we do not need to include this requirement explicitly. Note that we
cannot use the 6-neighbourhood for counting background components
as it is not 6-connected. The next largest choice is the 18-neighbour-
hood, which is indeed suitable for our task.

To summarize, we will use the following entities for characterizing
the topological classification of discrete binary images.

- $C^* :=$ number of 26-connected components of $N_{26}^*(x) \cap X$ that
  are 26-adjacent to x,

- $\bar{C} :=$ number of 6-connected components of $N_{18}(x) \cap \bar{X}$ that are
  6-adjacent to x.

Note that there may be 6-connected components of the background
that are not 6-connected to x as the example below shows. Here there
are three 6-connected background components within a 18-neighbour-
hood, of which only one is 6-adjacent to its centre.

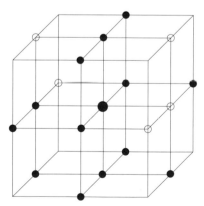

Using the same characterization as in table 4.1 we can identify the
topological type of most foreground voxels. However, some difficulties
remain. In particular, the identification of junction points is unsatisfactory, as the following example shows:

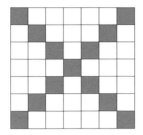 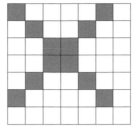 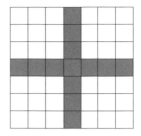

a) correctly classified   b) incorrect classification   c) incorrect classification

Here the centre voxels in b) and c) may be incorrectly classified as surface voxels rather than as junction points, while the junction in a) will be correctly labelled as a curve junction.

These problems can be easily rectified in a postprocessing step. We simply scan the classified image and reclassify every point that has more than two curve points in its 26-neighbourhood as a missed curve junction point.

Detecting simple surfaces

A more serious problem arises with regard to junctions between surfaces. Figure 4.5 shows examples of surface junctions. Using the definitions discussed so far we would correctly detect the junction points in the left image of figure 4.5 but fail to detect the ones in the right.

This problem relates to the problem of disconnecting a set of adjoining surfaces into what are called *simple surfaces*. One can think of simple surfaces as surfaces that do not connect to other surfaces. Removing all surface junctions from an image should therefore produce a set of simple surfaces. Let us try to give a more rigorous definition of simple surfaces.

Consider figure 4.6 which shows an object consisting of three simple surfaces indicated by three different shades of grey. The centre junction point belongs to all three simple surfaces.

Remember that surface points have exactly two background components and one foreground component. Let us now look at paths leading from one surface point to another. Note that the background components belonging to the points along the path form two sequences of overlapping sets as long as the two points belong to the same simple surface. For instance, in figure 4.6 there is a "top" and a "bottom" sequence of background components connecting points A and B such

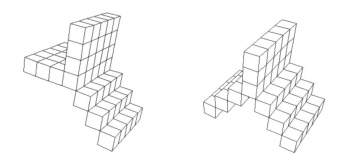

Figure 4.5: surface junctions

that adjacent components within this sequence overlap.

However, only one of the two sequences of background components leading from point A to D is a chain of overlapping sets. The "bottom" chain is disconnected at the junction point, indicating the fact that A and D belong to different simple surfaces. The following definition captures this idea.

Definition 4.1 Let X be some set of surface points. A sequence $(x_0, x_1, ..., x_n)$ of points in X is called a *simple surface path*, if the following two conditions hold:

1. x_i and x_{i+1} are 26-connected for any $i = 0, , , ., n - 1$;

2. for $i = 0, ..., n - 1$ let $B(x_i)$ and $C(x_i)$ denote the two background components of x_i. Then for all $i = 0, , , ., n - 1$ either

$$B(x_i) \cap B(x_{i+1}) \neq \emptyset \text{ and } C(x_i) \cap C(x_{i+1}) \neq \emptyset$$

or

$$B(x_i) \cap C(x_{i+1}) \neq \emptyset \text{ and } C(x_i) \cap B(x_{i+1}) \neq \emptyset.$$

The set X is called a *simple surface*, iff for any two points $x_0, x_n \in X$ there exists a simple surface path $(x_0, x_1, ..., x_n)$ in X connecting x_0 and x_n.

The above definition helps us to correctly identify junctions between surfaces such as the one in figure 4.5. The idea is to check the neighbourhood of each point initially labelled as a surface point and reclassify it as

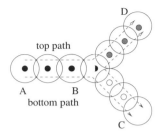

Figure 4.6: Identifying simple surfaces

a surface junction point if it belongs to more than two simple surfaces. This can be done by examining all surface points in its 26-neighbourhood. If there exist two surface points that cannot be connected by a simple surface path within the neighbourhood then the point in question must be a junction point. Note that this condition can only be checked within a $5 \times 5 \times 5$ window as we need to examine the background components that might extend beyond the initial 26-neighbourhood.

4.1.1 Algorithms for counting the number of connected components

The crucial part of topological classification is the calculation of the number of connected components in a small neighbourhood. Below we discuss a very simple but quite efficient algorithm for computing these numbers. In section 2.2 we have already introduced two different algorithms for computing connected components using either a depth search approach or a method based on equivalence tables. Clearly, we can use both algorithms for our present problem. However, employing the fact that we only need to consider a very small neighbourhood in which to search for connected components allows us to devise a much more efficient approach.

The basic idea is to precompute adjacencies that may occur within a k-neighbourhood and store these adjacency relations in a table. Thus, to compute the number of 6-connected background components in $\bar{X} \cap N_{18}$, we set up a two-dimensional array of size 18×6 in which the ith row contains the indices of all nodes 6-adjacent to node i, using a numbering such as the one shown below:

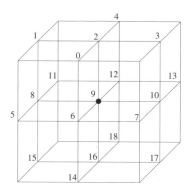

For example, node 5 has two 6-neighbours – {6, 8} – whose indices are stored in row 5 of the array.

The following algorithm which is listed in figure 4.7 expects a one-dimensional array called `inArray` of size 19 as input containing the binary input pattern whose connected components are to be counted. It will return the number of connected components as output producing an array `outArray` in the process which contains the corresponding component labels. The array `adjacency6[19][6]` contains the adjacency table described above, and `nadj6[19]` contains the number of 6-adjacent nodes for each row index in the table.

4.2   3D topological thinning

In many cases, we want to reduce the image content to its essentials. This is what topological thinning seeks to achieve. In thinning an image, we eliminate border voxels until only a skeleton of the original image remains. Figure 4.8 shows an example of such a process. Note that there are two different types of skeleton: the medial surface and the medial axis. In the following, we will discuss methods of obtaining such skeletons from a binary 3D image.

4.2.1   3D topology preservation

Suppose we have some arbitrary binary image that displays one or several connected components. The basic idea behind thinning is to delete as many voxels as possible from our binary image without destroying its topology. In addition, we also want to preserve its basic shape. The resulting image resembles a skeleton image.

```
int
VNumComponent6(VBit inArray[19])
{
   int outArray[19];
   int six[6] = {2,6,8,10,12,16};

   for (i=0; i<19; i++) outArray[i] = 0;

   label = 0;
   for (i=0; i<6; i++) {
      if (inArray[six[i]] == 0 || outArray[six[i]] > 0 ) continue;

      label++;
      outArray[six[i]] = label;

      n = 1;
      while (n > 0) {
         n = 0;
         for (j=i; j<19; j++) {
            if ((inArray[j] == 0) || (outArray[j] > 0)) continue;
            for (k=0; k<nadj6[j]; k++) {
               l = adjacency6[j][k];
               if (outArray[l] == label) {
                  outArray[j] = label;
                  n = 1;
                  goto next;
               }
            }
            next:  ;
         }
      }
   }
   return label;
}
```

Figure 4.7: Algorithm for counting connected components in a $3 \times 3 \times 3$ subimage

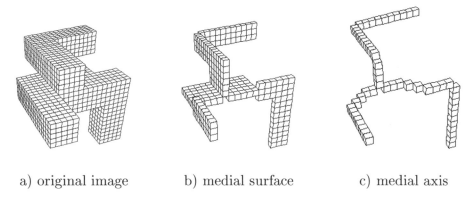

a) original image   b) medial surface   c) medial axis

Figure 4.8: 3D topological thinning

Recall from section 3.1 that two objects are topologically equivalent if their Euler number is the same. In other words, if we want to preserve the topology of our input image we must make sure that in the process of deleting voxels we do not accidentally disconnect formerly connected voxels, or connect unconnected ones. We also do not want to close cavities or handles or produce new ones.

Preserving topology is a minimum requirement for retaining shape information. In fact, topology alone is usually not sufficient to characterize the geometrical properties of an object. So for instance, any component that has no handles or holes is equivalent to a single voxel. If we were to delete voxels whenever the deletion preserves topology we would ultimately reduce every connected component to a single voxel. Thus, we need some further characterizations that prevent shrinking to a single voxel. Several such mechanisms exist which we will discuss in due course.

First, let us discuss the notion of *topology preservation* in more detail. Obviously, we do not want to compute the Euler number of the entire image each time we check a voxel to see whether it can be deleted without changing topology. We need some *local* criterion that can be checked in a small neighbourhood, preferably of size $3 \times 3 \times 3$ voxels. At first glance, this appears an impossible task. The reason is that connectivity is not a local property, as the following example shows [43]:

```
0  0  0  0  0        0  1  1  1  1        0  0  0  0  0
0  0  0  0  0        0  1  1  1  1        0  0  0  0  0
0 [0  0  0] 0        0 [1  0  1] 1        0 [0  0  0] 0
0 [0  0  0] 0        0 [1  x  1] 1        0 [0  0  0] 0
0 [0  0  0] 0        0 [0  0  0] 0        0 [0  0  0] 0
     slice 0              slice 1              slice 2
```

Note that the deletion of voxel x in slice 1 does not change the number of components in the entire image, even though it changes the number of components in a $3 \times 3 \times 3$ window surrounding x.

However, not all hope is lost. Even though connectivity is *not* a local property, topology preservation *is* local and can be recognized locally by inspecting $3 \times 3 \times 3$ neighbourhoods, as we shall see in a moment. Let us begin by defining topology preservation.

Definition 4.2 Let I be a 3D binary image. A point x in I is called a simple point, iff its deletion does not change the Euler number of I.

Recall from the previous section that we can identify topological types of voxels by inspecting the number of their foreground and background components. Fortunately, the topological type of "border voxel" which is identifiable by this method coincides with the notion of a simple point.

To see why, look again at table 4.1 of the previous section. Clearly, every other topological type listed in this table cannot be topologically simple. For instance, removing a surface point will produce a tunnel through the surface as surfaces are one-voxel thick sets. Also, removing junction points will create a hole or disconnect an object. Deleting an interior point will create an interior hole, and deleting an isolated point will reduce the number of connected components.

Note that topological classification is complete in the sense that every voxel receives some label, so that the only remaining candidate type for simple points is the border points. In fact, it has been shown[44], [45] that simple points and border points are indeed exactly the same. Thus, every border point is a simple point and vice versa.

Proof: We will just briefly sketch the proof here. For a complete reference see [44].

As before, let $\bar{C}(x)$ denote the number of background components and $C^*(x)$ the number of foreground components of a point x. Remember that border points have exactly one foreground and one background component.

It can be shown that for any point x in X the following holds:

1. $C^*(x) = 0 \iff$ a 26-component is removed by deletion of x.

2. $C^*(x) \geq 2 \iff$ a 26-component is created or a 26-handle is removed by deletion of x.

3. $C^*(x) = 0 \iff$ a 6-cavity is created by deletion of x.

4. $C^*(x) \geq 2 \iff$ a 6-cavity is removed or a 6-handle is created by deletion of x.

Thus, by 1. and 2. the deletion of x preserves the components and cavities. By 2. and 4. the handles of X and $\bar{x}$ are preserved, and by 3. and 4. the cavities of X and the components of $\bar{X}$ are preserved provided $\bar{C}(x)$ and $C^*(x)$ both equal one. $\square$

Earlier attempts at simple point definitions are given in [9], [33], [6], which we will not discuss here.

Clearly, we can use the algorithm discussed at the end of the previous section for counting connected components. Another algorithm can for instance be found in [46].

4.2.2 Thinning algorithms

Thinning algorithms proceed by iteratively deleting simple points which additionally fulfil some geometric constraints so that geometric features are retained. These algorithms differ in the order in which points are considered for deletion, and in the specific formulation of their geometric constraints.

From the previous discussion we might be deceived into believing that arbitrary deletions of simple points can do no harm to the topology of the image. However, beware of the disaster incurred by indiscriminately deleting simple points from the following image:

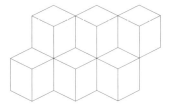

As you can easily check, *all* points in this image are simple. So if we were to delete all simple points simultaneously, the entire object would be erased! There are two different remedies that can be used here. The first – and simplest – remedy is to avoid simultaneous deletions altogether. Algorithms that employ this strategy are called *sequential thinning algorithms*.

In sequential thinning, only a single point may be deleted at a time. Sequential deletion of simple points has the advantage that the preservation of topology is always guaranteed. However, even a sequential algorithm would not really help here, as it would still eliminate all voxels except one.

The second class of algorithms allow simultaneous deletions of many simple points at a time, but not indiscriminately. These algorithms are called *parallel thinning algorithms*, as voxels may be deleted in parallel. Note that simultaneous deletions of simple points may destroy the topology of the image. Nonetheless, parallel thinning algorithms are quite popular, as they often yield better results provided some extra precautions are taken.

One such precaution may be to allow only certain types of deletion to occur in parallel. For instance, only voxels that belong to a "northern" border are deleted in parallel. Let us now formalize this idea a little further.

Definition 4.3 Let I be a 3D binary image, and let p be some black point in I. p is called a directed border point of direction N(orth), E(ast), W(est), S(outh), T(op), B(ottom), iff the point adjacent to p in direction N, E, W, S, T or B, respectively, is white.

Most parallel thinning algorithms work by allowing simultaneous deletions for each type of directed border point. The deletion of directed border points is often organized in subcycles, one for each of the six

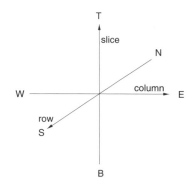

Figure 4.9: subcycle directions

principal directions (north, south, east, west, top and bottom). See figure 4.9 for our convention for the subcycle directions. All deletable border points in one direction are marked for deletion during a first scan through the image and then removed in parallel during a second scan. This entire process is repeated until no further deletions are possible.

There is one more point to consider. Recall from the introductory comments that we want to obtain a skeleton of the image which retains not only the topology of the image but also its basic geometric features. So for instance, if an object has two elongated branches then we want the resulting skeletonized object to retain these two branches, albeit in some thinned form.

In other words, our thinning algorithms need additional criteria for deleting points which prevent excessive shrinking. The basic idea is to identify end-points of branches and disallow their deletion even if these points happen to be simple points. The following definition clarifies this idea:

Definition 4.4 A simple point $x \in I$ is called a final point iff the number n of black points in its 6-(26-)neighbourhood is less than 2.

Note that if there are no adjacent black points (i.e. $n = 0$) then x is an isolated point. If $n = 1$ then x is an end-point of some branch or curve. In both cases, the deletion of x is not desirable.

Several thinning algorithms have been proposed in the literature, for instance [33], [47], [28], [43], [48], [49], [50] and others. We will now describe one of these algorithms in more detail, namely Tsao and Fu's algorithm [43] which was proposed in 1981.

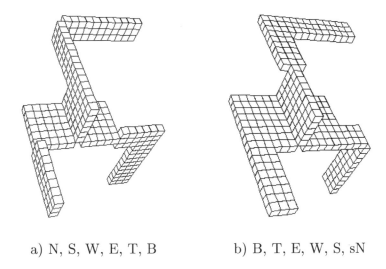

a) N, S, W, E, T, B   b) B, T, E, W, S, sN

Figure 4.10: different subcycle orders

Recall that there are two different types of skeleton: the medial surface skeleton, and the medial axis skeleton. In Tsao and Fu's algorithm we first compute the medial surface, and obtain the medial axis skeleton in a second pass. Let us first discuss the medial surface skeletonization.

The algorithm works by parallel deletion of directed border points that are simple and not final. The deletion of these points is organized in subcycles as described above. In addition to the simple point condition and the final point condition, this particular algorithm also uses a "checking plane condition" which ensures that the resulting skeleton is smooth.

It is tested in the following manner: for each subcycle the two checking planes are the 3 × 3 planes orthogonal to the current subcycle direction with the current voxel in the centre of that plane. The checking plane condition holds if the current voxel is "simple" in a 2D sense, i.e. if its deletion does not disconnect the remaining black voxels in the plane and the number of remaining black voxels is not less than 2. Below are examples of deletable and non-deletable points in the checking plane.

```
0 1 0          0 0 0
1 x 1          1 x 1
1 0 1          1 0 1
deletable      non-deletable
```

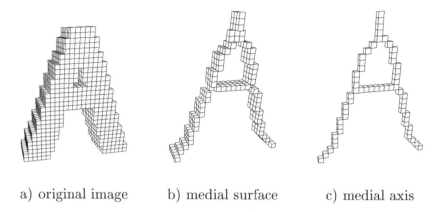

a) original image   b) medial surface   c) medial axis

Figure 4.11: 3D topological thinning using Tsao's algorithm

Unfortunately, the order in which the subcycles are executed is crucial. Figure 4.10 shows the thinning results with subcycle orders reversed when applied to the 3D image of figure 4.8.

Once the medial surface is extracted, we can then proceed to obtain the medial axis in a similar fashion. The only difference is that the checking plane condition is relaxed in this case. While in the medial surface case the number of remaining black voxels in the checking plane was required to be greater than 2, it now needs to be just greater than 1. Thus, to obtain the medial axis, we simply use the medial surface as input to the second stage of the skeletonization with the checking plane condition relaxed. Figure 4.11 shows results of both the medial surface and the medial axis skeletonization achieved by Tsao and Fu's algorithm using Bertrand's simple point condition.

A C-style version of Tsao and Fu's algorithm is given on the next page. Note that in the first step the raster addresses of all foreground voxels are stored in an array. Thus, we do not need to scan the entire image during each iteration to search for foreground voxels. During each subsycle, deletable voxels are marked for deletion by setting a flag, while the actual deletion is only carried out after all border voxels of the current subcycle direction have been inspected.

```
typedef struct {
   int b; /* slice index */
   int r; /* row index */
   int c; /* column index */
   int flag; /* deletion flag */
} Point;

VImage Thinning (VImage src) /* 3D thinning:  Tsao and Fu's algorithm */
{
   VImage dest; /* output image */
   Point addr[NMAX]; /* array containing raster addresses of all black pts */
   Copy(src,dest); /* copy the source image to the destination image */
   ndel = 1;
   while (ndel > 0) { /* loop until no further deletions possible */
      ndel = 0;
      for (dir=0; dir<6; dir++) { /* loop through 6 principal directions:  */
         db = 0; dr = 0; dc = 0;
         switch (dir) {
         case 0:  dr = -1; break; /* north */
         case 1:  dr = 1; break; /* south */
         case 3:  dc = -1; break; /* west */
         case 2:  dc = 1; break; /* east */
         case 4:  db = -1; break; /* above */
         case 5:  db = 1; break; /* below */
         }
         for (i=0; i<nblack; i++) { /* loop through all black points */

            /* skip if it has already been deleted:  */
            if (VGetPixel(dest,addr[i].b,addr[i].r,addr[i].c)) continue;

            /* skip if it is not a border point in the current direction:  */
            if (VGetPixel(dest,addr[i].b+bd,addr[i].r+dr,addr[i].c+dc) > 0)
               continue;

            /* if conditions satisfied, mark for deletion */
            if (NotFinalPoint(dest,addr[i].b,addr[i].r,addr[i].c,dir)
                and CheckingPlane(dest,addr[i].b,addr[i].r,addr[i].c,dir)
                and SimplePoint(src,addr[i].b,addr[i].r,addr[i].c))
               addr[i].flag = 1;
         }

         /* now delete all marked points in parallel:  */
         for (i=0; i<n; i++) {
            if (addr[i].flag -- 1) {
               VSetPixel(dest,addr[i].b,addr[i].r,addr[i].c) = 0;
               addr[i].flag = 0; /* reset the flag */
               ndel++;
            }
         }
      }
   }
   return dest; /* return resulting image */
}
```

∞   ∞   ∞   0   ∞   ∞   ∞   ∞   0   ∞

3   2   1   0   1   2   2   1   0   1

Figure 4.12: A 1D distance transform

4.3   Distance measurements

In many application domains it is essential to measure distances between objects. Suppose you have identified some relevant features such as a set of straight lines or a number of salient points in an image and now you want to measure how far away other parts of the image are from those features. Algorithms that solve such problems will be introduced in this section.

4.3.1   Distance mapping

Let us begin by looking at the simplest case, which is distance measurements along a one-dimensional line. Suppose that there is just one feature point on the line which is encoded by the number "0" since there is no "distance" to measure. The rest of the pixels on the line get an initial value of "infinity" to indicate that their distance to the feature point has yet to be determined. Algorithms for measuring the distance from feature points are called *distance transforms*. They produce a distance map in which each voxel receives a label indicating its distance from the nearest feature point. Figure 4.12 shows this arrangement together with the resulting distance encoded line, in which each pixel has received a distance label.

In the following, we will discuss algorithms for computing such distance maps. There are two major types of algorithm. The first type of algorithm computes exact Euclidean distances but is computationally expensive, while the second type of algorithm computes approximations to the Euclidean distances but works quite fast. We will begin with the second, approximate type of algorithm and deal with the more complicated but exact methods later.

Let us first look at the one-dimensional case to demonstrate the basic idea and then proceed to the two- and three-dimensional cases.

Distances within an image are global features which concern the entire image and not just small neighbourhoods. None the less, we would like to use local operations to measure them because we do not want to search through the entire image for a shortest path each time we need to measure a distance. Surprisingly, local computations suffice for estimating distances.

The basic idea is to propagate *local distances* in an iterative fashion until the entire image is processed. To see how this might work, let us again look at our simple example. Let

$$1 \quad 0 \quad 1$$

be a local mask representing local distances. The idea is now to move this mask over the entire image placing its centre on the current pixel. The local distance contained in each mask pixel is added to the current value of the corresponding underlying pixel. Finally, the value of the centre pixel is replaced by the minimum of all these sums. This procedure ensures that the local distances contained in the mask are propagated along the entire image, provided this operation is repeated for the entire image until each pixel has received a distance measurement. Imagine some "wavefront" emanates from the feature pixel and sweeps over the entire image, where the wavefront carries the distance measurement. Here are the first few iterations of this process:

$$\infty \quad \infty \quad \infty \quad 0 \quad \infty \quad \infty \quad \infty \quad \infty \quad 0 \quad \infty$$

$$\infty \quad \infty \quad 1 \quad 0 \quad 1 \quad \infty \quad \infty \quad 1 \quad 0 \quad 1$$

$$\infty \quad 2 \quad 1 \quad 0 \quad 1 \quad 2 \quad 2 \quad 1 \quad 0 \quad 1$$

The maximum number of passes required to label the entire line of pixels is limited by the greatest distance from the feature pixel. In the above example, three passes are necessary to complete the computation.

Note that this algorithm does not require any global search procedures as only local operations are used. However, it is still a somewhat tedious process as many passes over the entire image are necessary. Its advantage though is that the process can be performed in parallel. On a multi-processor machine each processor can work on some part of the image without having to deal with dependencies between pixels.

On single processor machines however, sequential algorithms are more useful. The basic idea behind sequential distance mapping is to split the wavefront emanating from the feature pixel into two (or more) directional waves. In the above example, we begin by letting a wavefront wash over the line from the left, which will produce distance measurements in the left to right direction. In a second (backward) step, a similar wavefront is pushed from right to left to produce right to left distances. In some places, the forward and the backward wavefronts meet. In those places, the minimum distance measurement wins. Below the sequential distance mapping is demonstrated for our simple one-dimensional example.

forward pass:

$$\infty \quad \infty \quad \infty \quad 0 \quad \infty \quad \infty \quad \infty \quad \infty \quad 0 \quad \infty$$

$$\infty \quad \infty \quad \infty \quad 0 \quad 1 \quad \infty \quad \infty \quad \infty \quad 0 \quad 1$$

$$\infty \quad \infty \quad \infty \quad 0 \quad 1 \quad 2 \quad \infty \quad \infty \quad 0 \quad 1$$

$$\infty \quad \infty \quad \infty \quad 0 \quad 1 \quad 2 \quad 3 \quad \infty \quad 0 \quad 1$$

$$\infty \quad \infty \quad \infty \quad 0 \quad 1 \quad 2 \quad 3 \quad 4 \quad 0 \quad 1$$

backward pass:

$$\infty \quad \infty \quad \infty \quad 0 \quad 1 \quad 2 \quad 3 \quad 4 \quad 0 \quad 1$$

$$\infty \quad \infty \quad 1 \quad 0 \quad 1 \quad 2 \quad 3 \quad 1 \quad 0 \quad 1$$

$$\infty \quad 2 \quad 1 \quad 0 \quad 1 \quad 2 \quad 2 \quad 1 \quad 0 \quad 1$$

$$3 \quad 2 \quad 1 \quad 0 \quad 1 \quad 2 \quad 2 \quad 1 \quad 0 \quad 1$$

Note that in the parallel algorithm, several passes over the entire image are necessary, where the number of passes depends on the greatest distance in the image. An update of distance values only takes place after an entire sweep over the image is completed. In the sequential case however, the number of passes is fixed and distance values are continually updated throughout each sweep.

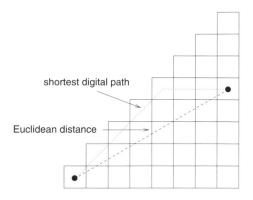

Figure 4.13: Digital paths in 2D

4.3.2 Measuring distances

We have seen that distance measurements play a central role in computing distance transforms. Before discussing two- and three-dimensional distance transforms, let us first discuss the more general problem of computing distances within an image lattice. Let us begin by looking at the two-dimensional case first before we proceed to three dimensions.

Distances in two dimensions

Distances between points are always defined with respect to some predefined metric. Usually, the Euclidean metric is used which measures the distance between two points (x_1, x_2) and (y_1, y_2) as

$$D_{euclidean}(x, y) = \sqrt{(x_1 - y_1)^2 + (x_2 - y_2)^2}.$$

Sometimes, it makes sense to use other metrics as well. The city-block metric for instance defines the distance between two points as the number of horizontal steps plus the number of vertical steps needed to connect the points. More formally, the city-block distance between x and y is defined as:

$$D_{city-block}(x, y) = |x_1 - y_1| + |x_2 - y_2|.$$

Usually, we would like our distance transformation procedure to produce a distance map that shows the Euclidean distances.

However, computing distances in digital images is not trivial as the result depends critically on whether we compute distances irrespective of the underlying voxel grid, or whether we compute the length of the digital n-connected paths. Figure 4.13 illustrates this problem.

Clearly, the Euclidean distance between the two points equals $\sqrt{7^2 + 4^2} \approx 8.06$. Approximating this distance by adding up the local distances along the shortest digital 8-connected path which links the two points may lead to quite a different result depending on the values we choose for estimating the local distances between the 8-adjacent pixels along the path. [1]

The simplest approach would be to sum up the lengths of the vertical, horizontal and diagonal steps along the way. The length of both a vertical and a horizontal step is 1, the length of a diagonal step is $\sqrt{2}$. Thus, the length of the entire path from x to y is

$$D = m_1 + \sqrt{2} * m_2$$

where m_1 denotes the number of horizontal/vertical steps and m_2 denotes the number of diagonal steps. In the above example, the distance would be $4 + 3 * \sqrt{2} \approx 8.24$ which is much larger than the Euclidean distance.

A better approach would be to use other factors with which to approximate local distances. Let a denote the local distance in the horizontal/vertical direction and let b denote the local distance in the diagonal direction. These factors form a local distance map as follows:

$$
\begin{array}{ccc}
b & a & b \\
a & 0 & a \\
b & a & b
\end{array}
$$

Our aim now is to choose values for a and b such that the length of a digital path between x and y as measured by

$$D = a * m_1 + b * m_2$$

approximates the "true" Euclidean length as closely as possible by computing values for a and b that minimize the difference between the Euclidean and the approximate metric. Several different approaches to

---

[1]Note in passing that there may be several digital paths of equal length connecting the two points. In fact, there even exist algorithms for counting the number of such shortest digital paths [51].

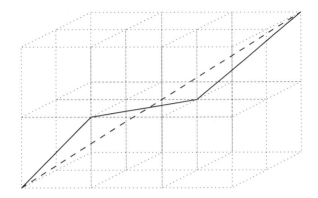

Figure 4.14: Digital paths in 3D

this optimization problem are conceivable. We will not go into more detail at this point. The interested reader is referred to [52] for further details. Borgefors [52] recommends using the following values for a and b:

$$a = 0.95509$$
$$b = 1.36930$$

The maximum error difference from the Euclidean distance is bounded by approximately $0.04491 * M$, where $M = \max\{|x_1 - x_2|, |y_1 - y_2|\}$.

A distance metric that approximates the Euclidean metric in the way described here is sometimes called a *chamfer metric* because the way the metric is defined reminds one of the process of chamfering a piece of wood by rounding off edges. Figure 4.17 shows the chamfer distances from a single foreground voxel. Note that voxels of equal distance from the centre voxel form a square that seems "rounded off" around the edges, which is due to the chamfering effect of this metric.

Distances in three dimensions

In three dimensions, the local distance map contains three values and stretches over three bands:

$$
\begin{array}{ccc@{\quad}ccc@{\quad}ccc}
c & b & c & b & a & b & c & b & c \\
b & a & b & a & 0 & a & b & a & b \\
c & b & c & b & a & b & c & b & c
\end{array}
$$

The Euclidean lengths for these values are:

$$
\begin{aligned}
a &= 1 \\
b &= \sqrt{2} \\
c &= \sqrt{3}.
\end{aligned}
$$

As in the two-dimensional case, using these values would lead to a consistent overestimation of distances as illustrated by figure 4.14. Again, we need to perform an optimization to find out which values yield the closest approximation to the true Euclidean distance. Several approaches have been reported in the literature [53], [54], [55]. Unfortunately, depending on the optimization criteria chosen, different values emerge. We will simply report them here, and leave it to the reader to check out the details from the literature.

	a	b	c
Borgefors [53]	1.0	1.314	1.628
Beckers [54]	0.8875	1.34224	1.59772
Kiryati [55]	0.9016	1.289	1.615
Verwer [56]	0.9398	1.3291	1.6278

Kiryati [55] points out that the problem of choosing optimal values for local distance maps to be used in distance transformations and the problem of choosing values for measuring the length of a digitized 3D line are not identical, and therefore different optimal values emerge for both problems.

4.3.3   Two-dimensional distance transforms

Let us begin with sequential distance transforms that are approximate versions of true Euclidean transforms. As noted in the introduction, the sequential algorithm uses two passes over the image, one going from the top left corner of the image towards the bottom right. The reverse pass begins in the bottom right corner and works its way up to the top left corner.

During each pass, a local distance map is moved across the image so that local distances are propagated along the way. We use different distance masks for the forward and backward passes. Below, the general layout of a forward and a backward mask are shown.

b	a	b		0	0	0
a	0	0		0	0	a
0	0	0		b	a	b
forward mask				*backward mask*		

Values for a and b are derived as described in the previous section, as the procedure amounts to adding local distances along digital paths. We may therefore use for instance $a = 0.95509$ and $b = 1.36930$ for the local distances as proposed by Borgefors [52].

At each step – say at pixel location r_0, c_0 – the following computation is performed:

$$pixel_{r_0,c_0} = \min\{mask_{r_0+r,c_0+c} + pixel_{r_0+r,c_0+c} \mid r,c = -1,0,1\}.$$

In other words, the current value of each pixel is added to the local distance value taken from the mask "above" it. The centre pixel is then replaced by the minimum of all these sums. Below a small example illustrates this step. During the first two rows the values are unchanged. As soon as the mask has passed a feature pixel, distances begin to add up. After a few steps the end of the first scan is reached and local distances in one direction have added up.

∞	∞	∞	∞	∞		∞	∞	∞	∞	∞
∞	∞	∞	∞	∞		∞	∞	∞	∞	∞
∞	0	a	∞	∞		∞	0	a	$2a$	$3a$
∞	a	b	∞	∞		∞	a	b	$(b+a)$	$(b+2a)$
∞	∞	∞	∞	∞		∞	$2a$	$(b+a)$	$2b$	$(2b+a)$

passing the first feature pixel   *reaching the end of the first pass*

To obtain even closer approximations to Euclidean distances larger neighbourhoods can be used. See [52] for more information on that subject.

4.3.4 Three-dimensional distance transforms

The distance transform carries over to the three-dimensional case in a more or less straightforward fashion. As before, we use local distance maps – this time three-dimensional – that are swept over the image to propagate distances. Again, we use two passes over the image, where

```
VImage ChamferDistance3D(VImage src)
{
    initialize the output image v_{b,r,c} by setting all foreground voxels
    to 1, and all background voxels to some very large number ("infinity")

    /*
    ** forward scan
    */
    for (b=0; b<nbands; b++) {
        for (r=0; r<nrows; r++) {
            for (c=0; c<ncols; c++) {
                if (v_{b,r,c} == 0) continue;
                v_{b,r,c} := min{v_{(b+i),(r+j),(c+k)} + forwardMask_{i,j,k}, -1 ≤ i,j,k ≤ +1}
            }
        }
    }

    /*
    ** backward scan
    */
    for (b=nbands-1; b >=0; b--) {
        for (r=nrows-1; r >=0; r--) {
            for (c=ncols-1; c >=0; c--) {
                if (v_{b,r,c} == 0) continue;
                v_{b,r,c} = min{v_{(b+i),(r+j),(c+k)} + backwardMask_{i,j,k}, -1 ≤ i,j,k ≤ +1}
            }
        }
    }
    return v }
```

Figure 4.15: Algorithm for computing a 3D chamfer distance transform

the first pass leads from the top left corner of the first slice towards the lower left corner of the bottom slice. The reverse pass begins at the lower left corner of the bottom slice and moves upwards toward the top left corner of the first slice.

At each step during the scan, the value at each mask position is added to the current value of the corresponding underlying pixel. The value of the centre pixel is then replaced by the minimum of all these sums. More precisely, let

$$
\begin{array}{ccc}
c \quad b \quad c & \quad b \quad a \quad b & \quad 0 \quad 0 \quad 0 \\
b \quad a \quad b & \quad a \quad 0 \quad 0 & \quad 0 \quad 0 \quad 0 \\
c \quad b \quad c & \quad 0 \quad 0 \quad 0 & \quad 0 \quad 0 \quad 0
\end{array}
$$

be the forward mask. The voxel value underneath the mask centre is replaced by

$$\min\{v_{(b+i)(r+j)(c+k)} + mask_{ijk} \mid -1 \le i, j, k \le +1, v_{(b+i)(r+j)(c+k)} > 0\}$$

where v_{brc} denotes the voxel value at the (band, row, column)-position (b, r, c).

Note that the values contained in the local distance mask are real numbers. Thus, floating point arithmetic is required throughout the process. As floating point arithmetic is usually slow, we may wish to speed up the computation by choosing integer valued distance masks. This can be easily achieved as follows [57]. Note that the ratio of the three values a, b, c contained in the mask is approximately

$$\frac{a}{b} \approx \frac{3}{4}, \quad \frac{b}{c} \approx \frac{4}{5}, \quad \frac{a}{c} \approx \frac{3}{5}.$$

Thus, by setting

$$a = 3, \quad b = 4, \quad c = 5$$

we approximately retain their respective ratios. Distance transforms using such values are sometimes called *weighted chamfer distance transforms*. Of course, the resulting distances in our distance map will be larger by roughly a factor of three, but we may rescale the distance map in a postprocessing step to obtain more accurate values. In figure 4.15 a C-style version of a three-dimensional distance transform using the chamfer metric is given.

4.3.5 Euclidean distance transform

So far we have discussed fast but only approximate methods. In the following, we will present a method proposed by Saito and Toriwaki [58] for computing exact Euclidean distance transforms. This method is somewhat slower than the preceding methods because it uses not strictly local computations, however, in cases where exact distances are required it is a good alternative. Other algorithms for computing Euclidean distance transforms are for instance [59], [60].

Saito's method uses three processing steps where in each step distances along one of the three principal directions are computed. Let us discuss each step in turn.

Transformation 1:

We begin by computing distances along the column direction as follows. Let

$$\{v_{b,r,c} \in \{0,1\} \mid 0 \le b < n_b, 0 \le r < n_r, 0 \le c < n_c\}$$

denote the three-dimensional binary input image, where n_b, n_r, n_c denote the number of slices, rows and columns, respectively.

In the first processing step, the input image is transformed voxel by voxel into an intermediate output image $f_{b,r,c}$ as follows.

Each background voxel $v_{b,r,c}$ is replaced by the squared minimum distance *within the same column* towards the closest foreground voxel, and the foreground voxels are left unchanged. More precisely, let $f_{b,r,c}$ denote the resulting output voxel, then

$$f_{b,r,c} = \min\{(c-j)^2,\ v_{b,r,j} = 0,\ 0 \le j \le n_c\}. \tag{4.1}$$

For instance, suppose the following input row is given:

1 0 0 1 0 0 0 0 0 1 1

After the first transformation this line is replaced by:

0 1 1 0 1 4 9 4 1 0 0.

Transformation 2:

For the second transformation, we scan the image produced in the first transformation column by column replacing each voxel by the following value:

$$g_{b,r,c} = \min\{f_{b,i,c} + (r-i)^2 \mid 0 \le i \le n_r\}. \tag{4.2}$$

Let us look at a small example. The first two transformations discussed so far have produced the following intermediate result:

0	0	0	0	0		1	4	9	4	1		1	2	5	4	1
1	0	0	0	0		0	1	4	4	1		0	1	4	4	1
0	0	0	0	0		1	4	9	4	1		1	2	5	2	1
0	0	0	0	1		1	4	4	1	0		1	4	4	1	0
0	0	0	0	0		1	4	9	4	1		1	4	5	2	1
original image						first transformation						second transformation					

To illustrate the second transformation, let us take a closer look at the second column. The second transformation of this column was computed as follows:

$$
\begin{aligned}
2 &= \min\{4 + (0-0)^2, 1 + (0-1)^2, 4 + (0-2)^2, 4 + (0-3)^2, 4 + (0-4)^2\}\\
1 &= \min\{4 + (1-0)^2, 1 + (1-1)^2, 4 + (1-2)^2, 4 + (1-3)^2, 4 + (1-4)^2\}\\
2 &= \min\{4 + (2-0)^2, 1 + (2-1)^2, 4 + (2-2)^2, 4 + (2-3)^2, 4 + (2-4)^2\}\\
4 &= \min\{4 + (3-0)^2, 1 + (3-1)^2, 4 + (3-2)^2, 4 + (3-3)^2, 4 + (3-4)^2\}\\
4 &= \min\{4 + (4-0)^2, 1 + (4-1)^2, 4 + (4-2)^2, 4 + (4-3)^2, 4 + (4-4)^2\}.
\end{aligned}
$$

Note that voxels touching the border in the column direction receive a distance value of 1, as this algorithm assumes that voxel sites not belonging to the address space of the image are also feature points. Therefore, the algorithm computes the distance to either the nearest feature point or the image border and outputs the smallest of the two values. If this is undesirable, a slight modification suffices to remedy this problem.

The second transformation yields a band-wise two-dimensional distance transformation of the squared Euclidean distances as you can see from the above example. Let us discuss why this is so.

Remember that according to equation 4.1 the first transformation yielded the squared distance to the closest feature voxel in the same row. Substituting equation 4.1 into equation 4.2 gives:

$$
\begin{aligned}
g_{b,r,c} &= f_{b,i,c} + \min\{(r-i)^2 \mid 0 \le i \le n_r\}\\
&= \min\{(c-j)^2 \mid v_{b,r,j} = 0, \ 0 \le j \le n_c\}\\
&\quad + \min\{(r-i)^2 \mid 0 \le i \le n_r\}\\
&= \min\{(r-i)^2 + (c-j)^2 \mid v_{b,i,j} = 0, 0 \le i \le n_r, 0 \le j \le n_c\},
\end{aligned}
$$

which is of course the squared Euclidean distance to the nearest feature point.

Transformation 3:

The third transformation computes distances along the third principal direction. It is a straightforward adaptation of the second transformation:

$$
h_{b,r,c} = \min\{g_{k,r,c} + (b-k)^2 \mid 0 \le k \le n_b\}. \tag{4.3}
$$

As we can readily check by substituting equation 4.2 into equation 4.3, this last transformation yields the three-dimensional Euclidean

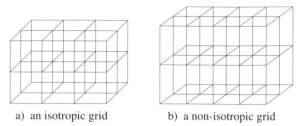

a) an isotropic grid   b) a non-isotropic grid

Figure 4.16: Isotropy of grids

distance transform.

$$
\begin{aligned}
h_{b,r,c} &= \min\{g_{k,r,c} + (b-k)^2 \mid 0 \le k \le n_b\} \\
&= \min\{(r-i)^2 + (c-j)^2 \mid v_{b,i,j} = 0, 0 \le i \le n_r, 0 \le j \le n_c\} \\
&\quad + \min\{(b-k)^2 \mid 0 \le k \le n_b\} \\
&= \min\{(b-k)^2 + (r-i)^2 + (c-j)^2 \mid v_{k,i,j} = 0, \\
&\qquad 0 \le k \le n_b, 0 \le i \le n_r, 0 \le j \le n_c\}.
\end{aligned}
$$

4.3.6   Non-isotropic voxel grids

In our discussion of distance transforms so far we have always assumed that the voxel grid is isotropic in the sense that distances between adjacent voxel locations are the same in all three principal directions. However, this is not always a realistic assumption. Quite often – especially in three-dimensional images – voxel grids have a different resolution in their slice direction than in their row or column direction. Clearly, distance transform algorithms must take account of this.

Figure 4.16 shows an isotropic and a non-isotropic grid in which the inter-slice distance is larger than the inter-row and the inter-column distance.

Saito's algorithm can be easily adapted to the non-isotropic case. All we need to do is to replace the previous three transformation equations by the following three equations:

Transformation 1':

$$
f_{b,r,c} = \min\{\alpha \, (c-j)^2 \mid v_{b,r,j} = 0, \ 0 \le j \le n_c\} \tag{4.4}
$$

Transformation 2':

$$g_{b,r,c} = \min\{ f_{b,i,c} + \beta\,(r-i)^2 \mid 0 \leq i \leq n_r\} \qquad (4.5)$$

Transformation 3':

$$h_{b,r,c} = \min\{g_{k,r,c} + \gamma\,(b-k)^2 \mid 0 \leq k \leq n_b\}. \qquad (4.6)$$

The parameters α, β, γ denote the distances between adjacent column, row and slice positions.

Adjusting chamfer distance transforms to account for the anisotropy of the voxel grid is just as easy. All we have to do is to adjust the values in our local distance mask accordingly.

Figure 4.17 illustrates the difference between the chamfer and the Euclidean distance transform. In 4.17b points of equal *3D chamfered distance* from the centre point are shown in cross-section. In 4.17c points of equal *3D Euclidean distance* are shown. Note that the 3D chamfer distance produces a hexagonal shape to approximate a sphere.

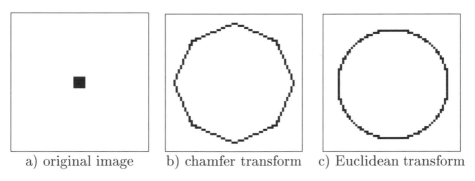

a) original image   b) chamfer transform   c) Euclidean transform

Figure 4.17: Different distance metrics

4.4 Medial axis transforms

In the preceding sections we have discussed thinning algorithms and distance transforms. In this section, we will show that there is a close relation between both types of algorithm.

Remember that in topological thinning we aimed at reducing a binary object to a stick-like figure that resembles a skeleton. We obtained the skeleton by successively eroding voxels along the object's border

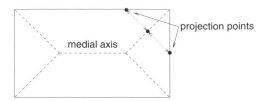

Figure 4.18: Medial axis transform of a box figure

until one-voxel thick surfaces or lines remained. The skeleton should reside in the object's centre so that its most salient features are retained. It is this particular feature that establishes a link to distance transforms. Clearly, the object's centre coincides with points having maximal distance from the object's borders.

An alternative way of computing an object's skeleton might therefore be the following. We first invert the image so that the background becomes the new foreground and vice versa, and compute the distance transform of the inverted image. The local maxima of the transformed image will represent points on the object's skeleton. Figure 4.18 illustrates this idea. In order to distinguish this type of algorithm from topological thinning we will henceforth call it the *medial axis transform*.

Unfortunately, things are not quite that easy, as a skeleton obtained in this fashion will probably not be topologically correct, i.e. it will not necessarily have the same Euler number as the original object. The reason is that local maxima of the distance transform are not guaranteed to form one voxel thick connected surfaces or strings of voxels. In fact, the critical part of medial axis transforms is the detection of local maxima of the distance transform followed by methods to achieve topology preservation.

Numerous approaches for this problem exist for two-dimensional images (for instance [61], [62], [63]). Much less research effort has been put so far into the three-dimensional case, although a few approaches exist[64], [65]. Historically, medial axis transforms go back to Blum's original *grassfire transform* [66]. Blum's idea was to describe the medial axis by a grassfire analogy: imagine that the borders of an object are starting points of fires eating their way towards the objects interior. The place where the firefronts meet coincides with the medial axis.

In the following, we will briefly describe the principal idea underlying medial axis transforms. For more detailed accounts see [64], [65]. A

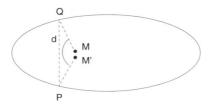

Figure 4.19: Computing the medial axis

fundamental property of points on the skeleton is that each skeleton is equally distant from at least two different points on the object border. Figure 4.18 illustrates this: for any point which is *not* on the skeleton there exists exactly *one* border point closest to it. Points on the skeleton however project to at least two points on the border. The border points closest to an interior point are called the *projection points* of the interior point. Projection points can be obtained from the distance transform. Daniellson's distance transform algorithm [59] directly supplies this information along with the distance measurements. The other algorithms we have discussed in the previous section are not that helpful in this regard. However, the projection points can be easily computed from the distance map using some simple search procedure.

The number of projection points is an important clue in identifying skeleton points. However, owing to the discrete nature of the voxel grid, a simple count of projection points is not usually feasible, as a skeleton point rarely coincides exactly with a lattice point on the grid. Therefore, we must compute projection points in a small neighbourhood. If two adjacent points in the neighbourhood project to two entirely different points on the border, then we may assume that the skeleton passes through those two interior points. Figure 4.19 shows how we can determine whether the two projection points are truly different. Both the angle spanned between the interior points M and M' and their projections P and Q as well as the distance between P and Q is indicative.

Using the above criterion we can identify good candidate skeleton points. However, the resulting skeleton is still not guaranteed to be topologically correct. Fernandez et al. [64] expand the above idea to solve this problem. We will not go into more detail at this point.

Finally, we should note that there exist entirely different approaches to medial axis extraction based on a concept from computational geom-

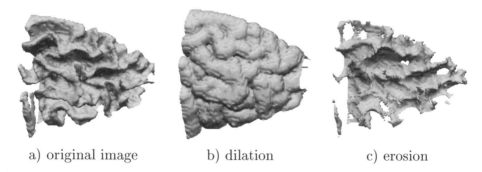

| a) original image | b) dilation | c) erosion |

Figure 4.20: 3D morphological operators (surface renderings)

etry called *Voronoi parcellation.* Voronoi parcellations have been used for 2D and 3D medial axis transforms [67], [68], [69]. In addition, a concept called *cores* which is related to the concept of medial axes has been developed by Pizer and others [70].

4.5   Binary morphology

Binary morphology opens another approach to analysing binary images. It has gained a lot of interest in recent years, especially through the seminal work of Serra [71] and Matheron [72]. A complete exposition of morphology is beyond the scope of this book, however, we will present a short review of the most basic concepts. Morphology provides a mathematically rigorous approach to many problems involving the description of shape and geometrical structure.

Its mathematical formulation easily generalizes to n-dimensions, so that in presenting the basic definitions we will generally talk about n-dimensional images. However, some applications in three-dimensional image analysis make morphology particularly attractive in comparison to alternative approaches. These applications will therefore be presented in more detail. Further information about morphology can be found in the following references: [71], [72], [4, pp. 157–261], [73], [74], [75], [76].

4.5.1 Basic definitions

Mathematical morphology provides two elementary operations called *dilation* and *erosion* which serve as a basic building block for a number of more complicated operators. Let us begin by first presenting the basic definitions of these two atomic operators before moving on to the more complex ones.

Let X denote a binary n-dimensional raster image defined on some lattice L, and let B denote a second binary image usually of much smaller size than X. Both X and B are assumed to be given in a set representation such that the sets X and B contain the raster addresses of all their foreground voxels.

In the following, B will be called the *structuring element*. Both dilation and erosion work by moving the structuring element B across the entire image while performing some set-theoretic operations to be defined below involving both X and B.

The process of moving the structuring element across the image can be described using the concept of a *vector translation*. A vector translation $X \pm b$ is obtained by shifting the addresses of all foreground voxels by some constant b:

$$X \pm b \stackrel{\text{def}}{=} \{x \pm b \mid x \in X\}.$$

We are now ready to define the concept of dilation and erosion as follows:

Definition 4.5 The *dilation* of a binary image X using the structuring element B is defined as:

$$X \oplus B \stackrel{\text{def}}{=} \bigcup_{b \in B} X + b = \{x + b \mid x \in X, \ b \in B\}.$$

The *erosion* of a binary image X using the structuring element B is defined as:[2]

$$X \ominus B \stackrel{\text{def}}{=} \bigcap_{b \in B} X - b = \{z \mid (B + z) \subseteq X\}.$$

---

[2]In some texts [71], the erosion operation is defined in a slightly different way using a *reflected* version of B such that $X \ominus B = \bigcap_{b \in \check{B}} X - b$, where $\check{B} = \{-b \mid b \in B\}$.

a) original image   b) opening   c) closing

Figure 4.21: 3D morphological operators (surface renderings)

Clearly, the result of a dilation or erosion operator critically depends on the choice of the structuring element. In three-dimensional morphology, we mostly use sphere-shaped structuring elements of various sizes. However, any arbitrary shape may be used depending on the type of problem at hand.

Figure 4.20 for instance shows the results of a dilation and an erosion operation where for the dilation a sphere of diameter 9 was used as structuring element, and for the erosion a sphere of diameter 5 was used. Note that the dilation "dilates" or expands the original image so that the canyons are filled and the hill tops grow, whereas the erosion "erodes" or shrinks the image so that the canyons are widened and the hills are diminished.

Other three-dimensional structuring elements that are often used are cones, boxes, pyramids or cylinders. Cylinders and cones are primarily used when the stack of slices represents a time series or a "movie" consisting of several images through time. A cone whose principal axis is parallel to the time axis may then allow tracking of some object through the time slices. And as time progresses, the radius of the cone widens so that deviations from the initial location can be accounted for.

While dilations and erosions as the elementary operations are quite useful in their own right, they are most often used in conjunction with one another or with other image processing routines. The most frequently used operations are called *opening* and *closing*, which are defined as follows.

Definition 4.6 The *opening* of an image X with a structuring element B is obtained by first eroding and then dilating X with B:

$$X \circ B \stackrel{\text{def}}{=} (X \ominus B) \oplus B.$$

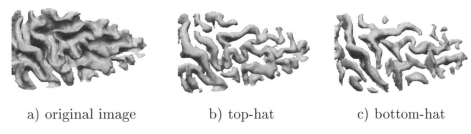

| a) original image | b) top-hat | c) bottom-hat |

Figure 4.22: 3D morphological operators (surface renderings)

The *closing* of an image X with a structuring element B is obtained by first dilating and then eroding X with B:

$$X \bullet B \overset{\text{def}}{=} (X \oplus B) \ominus B.$$

Figure 4.21 shows the effect of opening and closing operations using a sphere-shaped structuring element. Note that in contrast to the dilation operator, the closing operator only fills the canyons but does not cause the hilltops to rise. This is achieved by the subsequent erosion process which removes the "coating" from the hilltops.

4.5.2 Applications of morphological filters

Morphology can be used for a large number of different applications. For instance, a noisy surface may be smoothed by a morphological closing using a small sphere-shaped structuring element. Alternatively, spurious noisy parts can be disconnected from a surface using a morphological opening. Connected components labelling followed by a removal of small components eliminates these parts.

Identifying peaks and valleys

Morphological transformation can even be used to detect curvature types such as convexity or concavity. The basic idea is the following: concavities are defined as indentations in the surface that can be filled by a closing operator. Therefore, we can extract concave regions by subtracting the original binary image from the closed image. This operation is sometimes called a *bottom-hat transformation* because it finds the valleys or bottoms of a surface shaped like a hat.

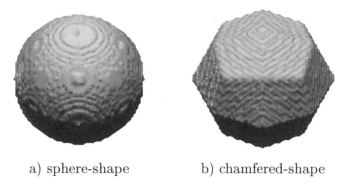

a) sphere-shape   b) chamfered-shape

Figure 4.23: Structuring elements (surface renderings)

Likewise, peaks can be discovered by first opening the image and then subtracting the opened image from the original image. This operation is called a *top-hat transformation* because it finds the "tops" of a hat or the peaks of a surface. Below, these two operations are defined formally.

Definition 4.7 The *top-hat transformation* is defined as:

$$X - (X \circ B).$$

The *bottom-hat transformation* is defined as:

$$(X \bullet B) - X.$$

Figure 4.22 shows the result of a top-hat and a bottom-hat transformation applied to our standard image.

In section 7.5, we will introduce an alternative method of classifying curvature types based on differential geometry. Differential geometry computation of curvature is based on second-order partial derivatives which are often difficult to obtain and are easily corrupted by noise. On the other hand, differential geometry provides a more sophisticated approach to curvature computation and allows a wider range of curvature measurements to be taken.

4.5.3   Morphology and distance transforms

Morphological filtering by a sphere-shaped structuring element can be simulated using a distance transform. Sometimes, especially for large

a) original image   b) border effects   c) no border effects

Figure 4.24: Removal of border effects of the closing operator

structuring elements, this approach can be implemented much more efficiently, so that it is quite often used in practice.

The procedure is the following: to simulate a morphological erosion we begin by inverting the input image so that the foreground voxels become background voxels and vice versa. We then apply a distance transform to the inverted image which computes to the background of the original image. Finally, we threshold the distance map so that only voxels at a certain distance from the background remain.

If we use a Euclidean distance transform, then our simulation procedure is equivalent to applying a morphological erosion with a sphere-shaped structuring element whose radius corresponds to the threshold used for the final step. Thresholding a chamfer distance map corresponds to using a hexagonal structuring element. Both types of structuring element are shown in figure 4.23. In principal, we could devise any number of structuring elements by using various local distance maps in our chamfer distance transform.

In a similar manner, morphological dilation can be simulated by thresholding a distance transform. Only this time, we do not need to invert the image first. Opening and closing operations require two applications of a distance transform each followed by a thresholding.

Note that some care must be taken to avoid strange effects around the image borders. Figure 4.24 shows the effect of a closing operation where the threshold of the distance map exceeds the image boundaries. The problem here is that in thresholding the dilated image, the image border is met so that the following erosion cannot fully recover the original object shape. To avoid such problems, special precautions must be taken. For instance, enlarging the image prior to the procedure will help.

4.5.4   Implementation

Volumetric images are usually quite large so that morphological filtering can take a long time. The speed of the computation depends on the type of data representation used. The easiest implementations are based on the raster representation, which in many cases is quite sufficient. Some improvement can be achieved by choosing a different representation for the structuring element. For instance, the structuring element may be represented as an array containing the addresses of all foreground voxels, while the original image is stored in raster format. Definitions 4.5 can then be directly translated into code.

More efficient implementations can sometimes be obtained by using one of the alternative representations introduced in section 2.3. The track representation for instance, is quite well suited to this task. Morphological operators are primarily based on shifting operations and the set operations "union" and "intersection". Shifting can be quite easily implemented in the track representations as all we have to do is to update the starting addresses. However, we must take special precautions at the image borders to prevent tracks from leaving the address space. Set operations such as union and intersection of tracks have also been discussed in section 2.3.

Octrees may also be a useful representation scheme in this context. Set operations can be quite efficiently implemented although shifting addresses in octrees can be awkward.

A general rule of thumb is that using a representation other than the standard raster format is only recommendable if this representation is also required for some further processing. Converting an image into either tracks or octrees for the sole purpose of morphological filtering is usually not efficient.

Part II

3D Grey Level Images

Chapter 5

Image enhancement

In this second part of the book we will discuss methods of analysing general grey level – not just binary – images. We begin by some simple methods of image enhancement that are useful for noise removal for instance, and then proceed to surface detection techniques. Surface detection plays an important role in the analysis of three-dimensional images as they delineate boundaries betwcen objects.

Let us begin with image enhancement methods. The goal of image enhancement is to prepare raster images for further processing or for display by removing noise or enhancing contrast. It is usually performed by applying some function to the image, so that the input image f is transformed into an output image g using a filter functional T:

$$T(f) = g.$$

We distinguish between linear and non-linear filters depending on whether T is linear or not. We will begin by discussing linear filters and then move on to some non-linear techniques. We will focus our presentation on three-dimensional raster images, although most filters that will be subsequently discussed here generalize easily to the n-dimensional case. Therefore, we will only give a brief overview here. Readers who are interested in more detail should consult one of the many excellent textbooks on this topic (for instance [1], [4]).

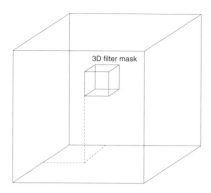

Figure 5.1: A 3D filter kernel

5.1   Convolutions

Perhaps the easiest method of noise cleaning consists in simply replacing each voxel by the average of the voxel values in some small neighbourhood around it. Sometimes, we want to improve this procedure by using a weighted average, so that voxels closer to the current voxel receive a higher weight in the averaging process. In 3D, this amounts to first creating a filter mask of some small size – say $5 \times 5 \times 5$ voxels – which contains the weights to be used for averaging, and then moving this mask across the image while replacing each voxel at location (b, r, c) by a weighted sum (see figure 5.1):

$$g_{b,r,c} = \alpha \sum_{i=-n}^{n} \sum_{j=-n}^{n} \sum_{k=-n}^{n} mask_{i,j,k}\; f_{b+i,r+j,c+k},$$

where α is some normalization factor. Such a procedure is called a *convolution*. It represents a linear filtering process in which the filtering functional is given by the filter mask.

One of the most commonly used filter mask is the *box filter*, in which all entries are equal to 1. More useful though is the *Gaussian filter*, whose mask entries are largest in the mask centre and drop off towards the mask borders. We will discuss Gaussian filters in more detail in section 7.2.1.

Convolution using filter masks represents the discrete version of continuous convolution which is defined as follows.

Definition 5.1 Let $U \subset \mathbb{R}^n$ be a bounded subset of $\mathbb{R}^n$, and let $g, h : U \to \mathbb{R}$ be two continuous functions defined on U. Then the *convolution* of g and h is defined as:

$$(g * h)(x) = \int_{\mathbb{R}^n} g(y) h(x - y) \, dy.$$

Fourier transforms

Convolutions can be used for a variety of purposes such as smoothing, noise cleaning, edge enhancement and even texture enhancement. Clearly, we must use different filter masks for each of these problems. The design of suitable filter masks therefore poses an important problem that must be addressed before convolution can be successfully put to work. A powerful method of filter design makes use of the close relationship between convolutions and Fourier transforms. In the following, a brief exposé of Fourier transforms will be given. A more detailed account can be found in many textbooks (e.g. [77]). Let us begin with the central definitions:

Definition 5.2 Let $U = \{x \in \mathbb{R}^n \mid \| x \| < B\}$ be a bounded subset of $\mathbb{R}^n$. The *Fourier transform* $\hat{f}$ of a function $f : U \to \mathbb{R}$ is defined as:

$$\hat{f}(\xi) = \frac{1}{(2\pi)^{n/2}} \int_{\mathbb{R}^n} f(x) e^{2\pi i x \cdot \xi} dx.$$

The *inverse Fourier transform* $\tilde{f}$ is defined as:

$$\tilde{f}(x) = \frac{1}{(2\pi)^{n/2}} \int_{\mathbb{R}^n} f(\xi) e^{-2\pi i x \cdot \xi} d\xi.$$

The inverse Fourier transform can be used to recover the original function:

$$\tilde{\hat{f}}(x) = f(x), \ \forall x \in \mathbb{R}^n .$$

The result of a Fourier transform is a complex function consisting of a real and an imaginary component:

$$\hat{f}(\xi) = \widehat{re}(\xi) + \widehat{im}(\xi).$$

In image analysis, we are often interested in the amplitude at each frequency, which is given by the *power spectrum*. It is defined as

$$\| \hat{f}(\xi) \|^2 = \widehat{re}^2(\xi) + \widehat{im}^2(\xi).$$

The *phase* is less often used. It is defined as:

$$\phi(\xi) = \arctan \frac{\widehat{im}(\xi)}{\widehat{re}(\xi)}.$$

The connection between the Fourier transform and convolution is given by the *convolution theorem* which states that convolving a function with another function and then applying the Fourier transform is equivalent to multiplying the Fourier transforms of both functions:

$$\widehat{(f * h)} = \frac{1}{(2\pi)^{n/2}} \, \widehat{f} \, \widehat{h}.$$

This fact can be used in designing convolution filter masks. For instance, we often want to remove high-frequency noise from an image such that only low frequencies remain. Such filters are called *low-pass filters* because they allow low frequencies to pass through. In the frequency domain, the design of such a filter is quite easy. Let

$$g(\xi) = \begin{cases} \| \, \xi \, \|, & \text{if } \| \, \xi \, \| \le b, \\ 0, & \text{otherwise.} \end{cases}$$

Then, by the convolution theorem, the Fourier inverse of g is a filter kernel suitable for low-pass filtering. However, this particular filter kernel is really not the best choice conceivable. For more on the use of the Fourier transform as a method of filter design see for instance [78].

Separability

In the context of volumetric images, we are particularly concerned with the computational burden associated with applying convolutions. In some cases, the convolution theorem can help to pave the way to more efficient implementations. The idea is the following: suppose a filter kernel h can be separated into two components such that

$$h = h_1 * h_2.$$

Then,

$$\widehat{(f * (h_1 * h_2))} = \widehat{f} \cdot \widehat{(h_1 \cdot h_2)} = \widehat{(f * h_1)} \cdot \widehat{h_2} = \widehat{((f * h_1) * h_2)}.$$

Thus, convolution is an associative operation. In other words, instead of applying the entire kernel h at one time, we can separate the application of h into two phases, where in the first phase only h_1 is applied to the image, and then h_2 is applied to the convolved image. The computational load can be enormously reduced by splitting the convolution process in this manner if the two separate kernels have a lower dimension. For instance, if h is a three-dimensional kernel that can be separated into three one-dimensional kernels, then the speed-up is as follows.

A conventional convolution using a 3D filter mask of size $n \times n \times n$ requires n^3 multiplications and $n^3 - 1$ additions per voxel. In contrast, a convolution separated into three one-dimensional components requires only $3n$ multiplications plus $3(n-1)$ additions.

5.2 Non-linear Filters

Convolution filters do not always produce satisfactory results. In particular, simple smoothing using a linear filter often leads to a blurring of edges and thus to a considerable loss of information. In the following, a few edge-preserving filters will be introduced. Edge preserving can only be achieved by non-linear filters, which is why we now move on to non-linear filtering.

The Median Filter

A well known method of edge-preserving smoothing is called *median filtering* [79]. The method works by replacing each voxel by the *median* of its surrounding voxels. The median is obtained by sorting the grey values of the $k = m \times m \times m$ voxels within the subimage and taking the value at the $k/2$th position in the sorted list.

The median filter has the advantage of preserving the set of grey values of the original image by not introducing any new intermediate values. It also has edge-preserving qualities.

The Sigma Filter

Better results are usually obtained by the *sigma filter* [80] which provides a very simple but effective method of edge-preserving smoothing. It can be implemented as a slight variation of the box or Gaussian filter. Just as in linear filtering, a filter kernel is moved across the image

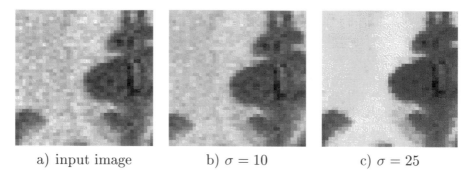

a) input image   b) $\sigma = 10$ c) $\sigma = 25$

Figure 5.2: Sigma filtering

and a weighted average is computed using the filter mask. However, in contrast to standard convolutions, only those voxels whose grey values do not deviate too much from the centre voxel are permitted into the averaging process. As a result, voxels which are located in areas of high grey value contrast – such as at boundaries between objects – are only slightly affected by the smoothing process, so edges are preserved. Figure 5.2 shows an example.

5.2.1   Anisotropic diffusion

Anisotropic diffusion [81] has gained a lot of attention recently as it has proved to be a powerful tool for image enhancement. The method has the advantage that it can be used for both smoothing and noise cleaning as well as edge enhancement. Gerig at al. [82] have generalized it to three-dimensional images.

The basic idea underlying the approach is that smoothing and edge enhancement can be modelled as a diffusion process in which a flow exists between adjacent cells containing substances such as gases or fluids. In our context, the cells correspond to homogeneous regions in the image that are separated by boundaries. As the diffusion process evolves over time, the homogeneity within those regions increases as small grey level variations are levelled out while at the same time the boundaries between regions become more pronounced.

Let $I(\bar{x})$ be the image intensity function, where $\bar{x} = (x_0, x_1, x_2)$ denotes some voxel location. For the moment let us assume that the voxel locations are defined in the continuous space rather than on a discrete lattice. In applying the diffusion model to an image I, a sequence of images $I_t, t = 0, 1, 2, 3, \ldots$ is produced, where I_0 equals the original image and the subsequent images are increasingly smoothed versions of I_0. Let us denote these images as $I(\bar{x}, t)$, assuming a continuous time parameter t.

From physics we know that diffusion processes of the type needed for our problem can be described by a partial differential equation of the form:

$$\frac{\partial I(\bar{x}, t)}{\partial t} = div(c(\bar{x}, t)\nabla I(\bar{x}, t)) \qquad (5.1)$$

where *div* denotes the *divergence operator* defined as

$$div f(\bar{x}) = \sum_{i=0}^{n-1} \frac{\partial f}{\partial x_i}$$

and ∇ denotes the gradient:

$$\nabla f(\bar{x}) = (\frac{\partial f}{\partial x_0}, \ldots, \frac{\partial f}{\partial x_{n-1}}).$$

The gradient of the image intensity function describes the amount of change from one voxel to the next. Thus, the gradient is large around boundaries between regions and it is small within regions. Image gradients and techniques of computing them are discussed in more detail in chapter 7.

The function $c(\bar{x}, t)$ is called the *diffusion coefficient*. In conjunction with the gradient it describes the *flow* between cells which is defined as:

$$\Phi = c(\bar{x}, t)\nabla I(\bar{x}, t).$$

The flow determines the amount of interchange between adjacent cells. If the diffusion coefficient is constant, i.e. $c(\bar{x}, t) = c$, then the flow is proportional to the gradient. Diffusion processes in which the diffusion coefficient is constant are called *isotropic*, otherwise they are called *anisotropic*.

Remember that our primary goal is to make homogeneous regions even more homogeneous. Therefore, we would like to have a strong flow within homogeneous regions and little or no flow across region boundaries. This can be achieved by using an appropriate function as

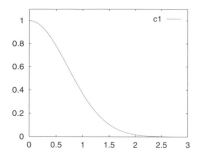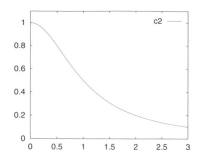

Figure 5.3: Diffusion functions

diffusion coefficient. Let us define $c(\bar{x}, t)$ as a function f of the gradient magnitude:

$$c(\bar{x}, t) = f(\| \nabla I(\bar{x}, t) \|).$$

Then f must be a monotonically decreasing function so that the flow increases within homogeneous regions where the gradient is small. The following two diffusion functions have been proposed by Perona et al. [81] (see figure 5.3):

$$c_1(\bar{x}, t) = exp(-(\| \nabla I(\bar{x}, t) \| /K)^2)$$

and

$$c_2(\bar{x}, t) = \frac{1}{(1 + \| \nabla I(\bar{x}, t) \| /K)^2}$$

for some parameters $K, \alpha > 0$.

The diffusion equation can be solved numerically in an approximate, iterative fashion as follows. First note that a gradient can generally be approximated by:

$$\frac{\partial f}{\partial x} = \frac{1}{\Delta x} \left[f(x + \frac{\Delta x}{2}) - f(x - \frac{\Delta x}{2}) \right]. \tag{5.2}$$

For simplicity, we first deal with the two-dimensional case. Using the above approximation, we get [82]:

$$\frac{\partial I(\bar{x}, t)}{\partial t} = div(c(\bar{x}, t) \nabla I(\bar{x}, t))$$

$$= \frac{\partial}{\partial x_0} \left[c(\bar{x}, t) \frac{\partial I}{\partial x_0} \right] + \frac{\partial}{\partial x_1} \left[c(\bar{x}, t) \frac{\partial I}{\partial x_1} \right]$$

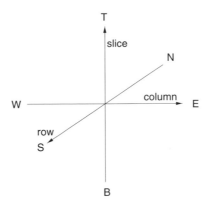

Figure 5.4: diffusion directions

$$\approx \quad \frac{\partial}{\partial x_0} \left[c(\bar{x},t) \frac{1}{\Delta x_0} \; I(x_0 + \frac{\Delta x_0}{2}, x_1, t) - I(x_0 - \frac{\Delta x_0}{2}, x_1, t) \right]$$

$$+ \quad \frac{\partial}{\partial x_1} \left[c(\bar{x},t) \frac{1}{\Delta x_1} \; I(x_0, x_1 + \frac{\Delta x_1}{2}, t) - I(x_0, x_1 - \frac{\Delta x_1}{2}, t) \right]$$

Let us use the following abbreviations:

$$d_i^+ \stackrel{\text{def}}{=} x_i + \Delta x_i, \quad \text{and} \quad d_i^- \stackrel{\text{def}}{=} x_i - \Delta x_i,$$

and also (see figure 5.4):

$$\Phi_E \quad = \quad \frac{1}{\Delta x_0^2} \left[c(x_0 + \frac{\Delta x_0}{2}, x_1, t)(I(d_0^+, x_1, t) - I(d_0^-, x_1, t)) \right]$$

$$\Phi_W \quad = \quad \frac{1}{\Delta x_0^2} \left[c(x_0 - \frac{\Delta x_0}{2}, x_1, t)(I(x_0, x_1, t) - I(x_0, x_1, t)) \right]$$

$$\Phi_N \quad = \quad \frac{1}{\Delta x_1^2} \left[c(x_0, x_1 + \frac{\Delta x_1}{2}, t)(I(x_0, d_1^+, t) - I(x_0, d_1^-, t)) \right]$$

$$\Phi_S \quad = \quad \frac{1}{\Delta x_1^2} \left[c(x_0, x_1 - \frac{\Delta x_1}{2}, t)(I(x_0, x_1, t) - I(x_0, x_1, t)) \right].$$

Then, after applying 5.2 one more time and some algebra the above equations simplify to:

$$\frac{\partial I(\bar{x}, t)}{\partial t} \approx \Phi_E - \Phi_W + \Phi_N - \Phi_S. \tag{5.3}$$

a) input image   b) after 7 iterations   c) after 15 iterations

Figure 5.5: Anisotropic diffusion

So that finally,

$$
\begin{aligned}
I(\bar{x}, t + \Delta t) \quad &\approx \quad I(\bar{x}, t) \; + \; \Delta t \, \frac{\partial I}{\partial t}(\bar{x}, t) \\
&\approx \quad I(\bar{x}, t) \; + \; \Delta t \, (\Phi_E \; - \; \Phi_W \; + \; \Phi_N \; - \; \Phi_S).
\end{aligned}
$$

The above formula describes the iterative process of anisotropic diffusion. At each new time step $t + \Delta t$, a new image is generated from the previous image of step t. The formula translates easily into the three-dimensional case. All we have to do is to enlarge the set of neighbouring voxels taken into account in the diffusion process. We can either use the 6-adjacent or the 26-adjacent voxels. For 6-neighbourhoods, the iteration formula is:

$$
\begin{aligned}
I(\bar{x}, t + \Delta t) \quad &\approx \quad I(\bar{x}, t) \\
&\quad + \Delta t \, (\Phi_E - \Phi_W + \Phi_N - \Phi_S + \Phi_T - \Phi_B).
\end{aligned}
$$

The 26-neighbourhood case is analogous. However, we should use some normalizing factors for the diagonal neighbours to account for their greater distance from the centre voxel. First note that as the voxel grid is discrete we may set $\Delta x = 1$ which represents the distance from one lattice point to the next. As the factor must equal $1/\Delta x^2$, we have $1/2$ for the 18-adjacent neighbours, and $1/3$ for the 26-adjacent neighbours. The choice of the time step size Δt is not quite so obvious. There is no lower bound on Δt. A small value of Δt gives a stable solution to the diffusion equation. On the other hand, a small Δt also entails that many iterations are required to achieve convergence. Gerig et al. [82] suggest the following values for Δt depending on the size of the neighbourhood system used.

dim	adjacency	max Δt
2D	4	1/5
	8	1/7
3D	6	1/7
	26	3/44

Chapter 6

Geometric transformations of voxel images

In this chapter, we will discuss geometric transformations such as scaling, rotating, or shearing of volumetric images. Such transformations are required in a number of circumstances. For instance, we may want to shift and rotate images into a standard position and orientation. In addition, we may need to change the resolution of the voxel grid to make it isotropic. All of these tasks require geometric manipulations of the voxel grid which we will now discuss.

6.1 Affine linear transformations

Suppose that we want to apply a linear transformation such as a rotation or a scaling to a 3D raster image. Such transformations may be given by a matrix of the form:

$$A = \begin{bmatrix} a_{00} & a_{01} & a_{02} \\ a_{10} & a_{11} & a_{12} \\ a_{20} & a_{21} & a_{22} \end{bmatrix}.$$

Unfortunately, we cannot simply apply this matrix to each voxel in the input image to obtain the new output image. To see why, suppose that the matrix performs a simple scaling by some factor, say three. The transformation matrix would then have the value "3" in all of its diagonal entries. Applying this matrix to the input image would yield an output image which is three times bigger than the input image, but which has many void places. All even numbered addresses in the output image would not receive a new value. One could argue that the output image should be produced by simply replicating each input value three times. But what would you do about non-integer scaling factors?

To circumvent such problems, we have to use a different approach. The basic idea is to successively fill in new values at each position within the output image. The value that a position in the output image should receive is obtained by computing a list of positions in the input image which correspond most closely to the "old" location, i.e the location prior to the geometric transformations and interpolating the values at those positions. To obtain these locations, we have to reverse the transformation by inverting the transformation matrix. Figure 6.1 illustrates this idea.

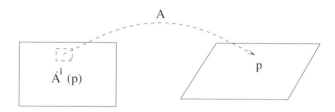

Figure 6.1: Resampling

Note that in most cases the inverted matrix will not yield valid integer addresses in the input image but instead some real-valued numbers which then have to be rounded off to produce valid raster addresses. Let us look at a small example to clarify this process. Suppose the transformation matrix performs a scaling by factor 3:

$$\begin{bmatrix} 3 & 0 & 0 \\ 0 & 3 & 0 \\ 0 & 0 & 3 \end{bmatrix}$$

Now suppose we want to compute the output value at raster position (10,20,16). Applying the inverse transformation yields:

$$\begin{bmatrix} 1/3 & 0 & 0 \\ 0 & 1/3 & 0 \\ 0 & 0 & 1/3 \end{bmatrix} \begin{bmatrix} 10 \\ 20 \\ 16 \end{bmatrix} \approx \begin{bmatrix} 3.33 \\ 6.66 \\ 5.33 \end{bmatrix}$$

The fact that the inverse transformation usually does not produce a valid integer address requires us to interpolate the values at the voxel addresses closest to the exact inverse address. Several different interpolation schemes have been used in the past. The most widely used is the so-called *trilinear interpolation* scheme. The basic idea is to sum up the values of the eight adjacent voxels, where each of the eight values is weighted according to its distance from the "true" location. Figure 6.2 shows this arrangement.

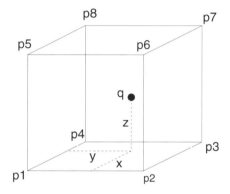

Figure 6.2: Trilinear interpolation

Let $p_i, i = 1, ..., 8$ denote the values at the locations closest to the inverse address. Let $q - (q_x, q_y, q_z)$ and $p_1 = (p_{1x}, p_{1y}, p_{1z})$, and

$$
\begin{aligned}
x &= |q_x - p_{1x}| \\
y &= |q_y - p_{1y}| \\
z &= |q_z - p_{1z}|
\end{aligned}
$$

be the Euclidean distances from the true location where q denotes the exact inverse address. With this notation, the interpolation formula is the following:

$$
\begin{aligned}
u = \ & x\,y\,z\,p_1 \ + \ (1-x)\,y\,z\,p_2 \\
& + x\,(1-y)\,z\,p_3 \ + \ (1-x)\,(1-y)\,z\,p_4 \\
& + x\,y\,(1-z)\,p_5 \ + \ (1-x)\,y\,(1-z)\,p_6 \\
& + x\,(1-y)\,(1-z)\,p_7 \ + \ (1-x)\,(1-y)\,(1-z)\,p_8.
\end{aligned}
$$

```
VImage TrilinearInterpolation(
   VImage src,        /* the input image                      */
   float a[3][3],     /* the transformation matrix            */
   float ainv[3][3]   /* the inverse transformation matrix */ )
{
   /* create a destination image of appropriate size */
   dest_nbands   = a[0][0] * src_nbands + a[0][1] * src_nrows + a[0][2] * src_ncols;
   dest_nrows    = a[1][0] * src_nbands + a[1][1] * src_nrows + a[1][2] * src_ncols;
   dest_ncolumns = a[2][0] * src_nbands + a[2][1] * src_nrows + a[2][2] * src_ncols;
   dest = VCreateImage(dest_nbands,dest_nrows,dest_ncols);

   /* loop through all voxels of the output image : */
   for (band=0; band<dest_nbands; band++) {
     for (row=0; row<dest_nrows; row++) {
       for (col=0; col<dest_ncolumns; col++) {

         /* apply inverse transformation to obtain source position : */
         band_pos   = ainv[0][0] * band + ainv[0][1] * row + ainv[0][2] * col + 0.5;
         row_pos    = ainv[1][0] * band + ainv[1][1] * row + ainv[1][2] * col + 0.5;
         column_pos = ainv[2][0] * band + ainv[2][1] * row + ainv[2][2] * col + 0.5;

         /* obtain coordinates of the closest voxels and clip to range:  */
         north  = (int) (band_pos);
         south  = (int) (band_pos) + 1;
         top    = (int) (row_pos);
         bottom = (int) (row_pos) + 1;
         left   = (int) (column_pos);
         right  = (int) (column_pos) + 1;
         clip_coordinates(&north,&south,&top,&bottom,&left,&right);

         /* obtain values of the eight closest voxels: */
         p1 = VGetPixel(src,north,top,left);
         p2 = VGetPixel(src,north,top,right);
         p3 = VGetPixel(src,north,bottom,left);
         p4 = VGetPixel(src,north,bottom,right);
         p5 = VGetPixel(src,south,top,left);
         p6 = VGetPixel(src,south,top,right);
         p7 = VGetPixel(src,south,bottom,left);
         p8 = VGetPixel(src,south,bottom,right);

         /* interpolate those values using trilinear interpolation: */
         x = (float) (right  - column_pos);
         y = (float) (bottom - row_pos);
         z = (float) (south  - band_pos);
         VSetPixel(dest,band,row,col) = x * y * z * p1  +  (1-x) * y * z * p2
            +  x * (1-y) * z * p3      +  (1-x) * (1-y) * z * p4
            +  x * y * (1-z) * p5      +  (1-x) * y * (1-z) * p6
            +  x * (1-y) * (1-z) * p7  +  (1-x) * (1-y) * (1-z) * p8;
       }
     }
   }
   return dest;  /* return the resulting image : */
}
```

On the previous page, an abbreviated C-style version of this algorithm is given. This algorithm can be used for any kind of linear transformation provided the transformation matrix is non-singular. The algorithm expects the original image and the transformation matrix and its inverse as input. It returns a destination image containing the transformed image. Figure 6.3 shows an image and its rotated version as an example.

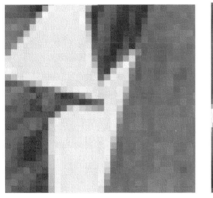 

a) original image   b) rotated by 20 degrees

Figure 6.3: Rotation of images (note the resampling effect)

6.2 Interpolation

In the previous section we discussed methods of performing affine linear transformations on a given three-dimensional raster image. In the following, we will discuss *interpolation* of such images, which in some ways may be seen as a special case of geometric transformations on images. Interpolation becomes necessary when the voxel grid of our raster image is not isotropic so that distances between lattice points are different in the three basic orthogonal directions. Figure 6.4 shows an example.

Recall from section 4.3 that the anisotropy of the voxel grid may cause problems in estimating distances between lattice points. There are many other image analysis routines which also depend heavily on the isotropy of the grid.

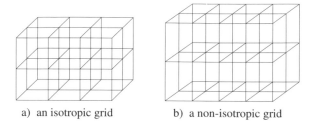

a) an isotropic grid   b) a non-isotropic grid

Figure 6.4: Isotropy of grids

There are various reasons why images are often acquired using aniso-tropic grids. Sometimes – especially in a medical context – it is nec-essary to minimize image acquisition time and dosage of radiation. In addition, the signal to noise ratio may be influenced negatively if slices are too thin.

Interpolation methods transform the image so that the resulting grid becomes isotropic. The general idea is to first define a new voxel grid and then fill in grey values at each lattice point by interpolating the values of the old grid. Various such methods exist, some of which we will discuss in the following. Interpolation methods can be roughly grouped into two main sections: the first group of methods perform an interpolation directly on the grey values using resampling techniques similar to the ones we discussed in the previous section.

The second group of techniques aims at preserving particular image features such as edges or homogeneous areas and thus requires some kind of feature extraction as a first step.

6.2.1 Interpolation of volumes

The easiest and also most frequently used interpolation method uses *trilinear interpolation* which we already discussed in the previous sec-tion. In the context of resampling a grid to make it isotropic, it is most often used with a transformation matrix of the form:

$$\begin{bmatrix} a & 0 & 0 \\ 0 & b & 0 \\ 0 & 0 & c \end{bmatrix}$$

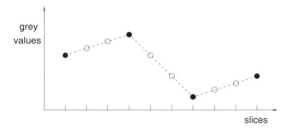

Figure 6.5: Linear interpolation

where a denotes the scaling factor for inter-slice distances, and b, c denote the scaling factor for the row and column directions. Figure 6.5 illustrates a linear interpolation between slices, if row and column distances are left unchanged. The black dots denote the grey values of the input volume and the white dots show the slices interspersed between them by the interpolation process. In this case, the number of slices is increased by an integer factor of three. Sometimes, greater smoothness can be achieved if cubic splines are used for interpolation (see figure 6.6). However, in most practical applications, linear interpolation is preferable because of its greater computational efficiency (see also [83] about interpolation kernels).

The sampling theorem

Clearly, we would like to know how good the interpolated volume represents the original "true" object. A simple, but quite effective method is to remove every second or third slice from a volume, apply an interpolation procedure in an effort to restore the original volume and

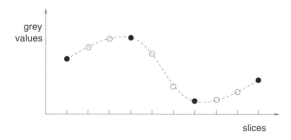

Figure 6.6: Spline interpolation

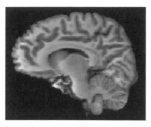 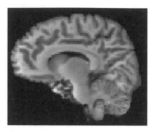

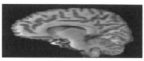

a) original image   b) scaled down   c) reconstructed image

Figure 6.7: Original volume and its interpolated versions

compare the results. If the interpolated image closely resembles the original image, then our interpolation scheme is satisfactory.

Figure 6.7 shows a magnetic resonance image of a human brain in both the original and the interpolated version. A close-up view (figure 6.8) reveals the differences between the two images. Note that the reconstructed image looks slightly blurred owing to the smoothing effect of the interpolation.

In addition to such heuristic considerations we would like to obtain an error assessment based on theory. A well known theorem from information theory – called the *sampling theorem* – helps to clarify this point. The sampling theorem states the following.

Let $f(x)$ be a continuous function which is sampled at regular intervals Δ, such that measurements are available at the following points:

$$f_n \;=\; f(n\Delta), \; n \;=\; ..., -3, -2, -1, 0, 1, 2, 3, ...$$

Then f can be completely reconstructed from its sampled measurements f_n, provided the spacing Δ is small enough and the function f is "smooth", where smoothness means that f is *bandwidth-limited*, i.e. its large frequencies determined by its Fourier transform must vanish.

More precisely, let $\widehat{f}$ denote the Fourier transform of f, i.e.

$$\widehat{f}(\xi) \;=\; \int_{\mathbb{R}^n} f(x) e^{2\pi i x \cdot \xi} dx.$$

Then f is called *b-bandwidth-limited*, iff

$$\widehat{f}(\xi) \;=\; 0, \quad \text{for} \quad \| \, \xi \, \| > b.$$

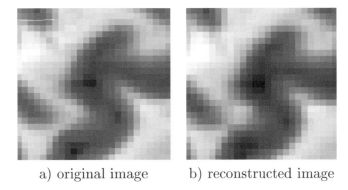

a) original image   b) reconstructed image

Figure 6.8: Close-up view of an interpolated volume

The sampling theorem now says, that a b-bandwidth-limited function f can be computed *at any point* from its sampled measurements by the formula:

$$f(x) = \Delta \sum_{-\infty}^{\infty} f_n \frac{2\pi b(x - n\Delta)}{\pi(x - n\Delta)} \tag{6.1}$$

provided the sampling rate is less than

$$\Delta = \frac{1}{2b}.$$

This sampling rate is sometimes also called the *Nyquist rate*.

In our context, this theorem prescribes the distances between lattice points on which grey values should be sampled, provided we somehow know whether the original image is bandwidth-limited. If such information is available, the interpolation formula is given by equation 6.1.

6.2.2 Feature-based interpolation

The interpolation techniques discussed so far do not take image content into account. While this is usually justifiable there are still some cases where more exact methods are called for. Figure 6.9 illustrates this point. Here many points belonging to an object interior are not detected in the interpolated slice as the interpolation scheme ignores relations between object boundaries in adjacent slices.

An obvious way round this problem is to first identify relevant features such as object boundaries and then match corresponding feature points in adjacent slices. A linear interpolation between corresponding

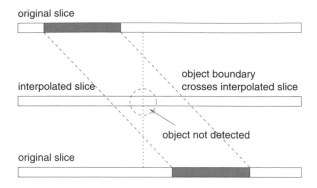

Figure 6.9: Object boundaries missed by linear interpolation

feature points will then produce the desired result. The most difficult part of this approach is of course the identification of suitable features and the detection of matches between them. Goshtasby et al. [84] have proposed the following features for matching:

- grey value,

- the norm of the grey value gradient,

- the direction of the gradient,

- the location within a slice.

0	1	1	1	1	1	1
0	0	0	0	0	1	1

a) the original image

0.5	-0.5	-1.5	-2.5	-3.5	-4.5	-5.5
4.5	3.5	2.5	1.5	0.5	-0.5	-1.5

b) the distance transformed image

0.5	-0.5	-1.5	-2.5	-3.5	-4.5	-5.5
2.5	3.0	1.0	2.5	-3.0	-2.0	-7.0
4.5	3.5	2.5	1.5	0.5	-0.5	-1.5

c) the interpolated image

Figure 6.10: Shape-based interpolation

A different approach – called *shape-based interpolation* – was pursued by Raya et al. [85]. They first segment the image so that foreground and background voxels are distinguished (see chapter 8 for segmentation techniques). In the second step, a distance transform is applied to this image, where distances are computed from object boundaries. Distance values corresponding to foreground voxels receive negative values and background voxels receive positive distance values.

The distance transformed image can now be interpolated using any standard interpolation scheme, for instance linear interpolation. Finally, the interpolated image is thresholded so that negative values become foreground voxels and positive values are attributed to the background. Figure 6.10 illustrates this procedure for one row where one slice is added by shape-based interpolation.

It is some disadvantage that this algorithm only works on binary images so that a segmentation becomes necessary. However, Grevera et al. have extended this scheme to grey level images [86].

Chapter 7

Surface segmentation

In this chapter, we will address the problem of extracting surfaces from three-dimensional image data sets. This problem is of great relevance for a number of reasons. The most obvious reason is that surfaces delineate object boundaries, and the ultimate goal of computer vision is to detect objects in images.

This chapter presents a "bottom-up" approach to detecting surfaces. We will start by identifying those voxels in the image which are candidates for being on object surfaces. We will then discuss methods of connecting those isolated voxels to larger conglomerates. Eventually, we will reconstruct larger surface patches from these conglomerates using higher-level representations.

7.1 Edges in 3D images

Before we enter the discussion of various boundary detection techniques, let us first clarify the notion of a "boundary" or an "edge" in a multi-dimensional image array.

First, assume that we have a one-dimensional continuous signal like the one shown in figure 7.1a. Clearly, there is a step at location zero in that signal. The position at which this step occurs marks a "boundary" between two events. We call this position an "edge". Unfortunately, signals are usually corrupted by noise, so that a more realistic situation is pictured in figure 7.1b. Edges that have profiles such as the one in figure 7.1a are called *step edges*. Other types of edge are also common in signals (see Figure 7.2).

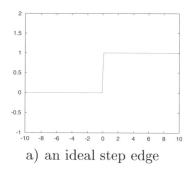

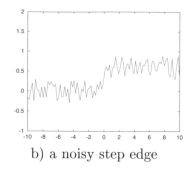

a) an ideal step edge   b) a noisy step edge

Figure 7.1: Step edges

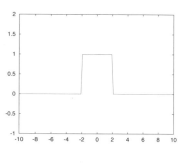

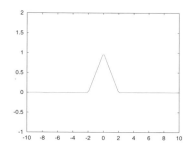

a) a ridge profile edge   b) a roof profile edge

Figure 7.2: Other edge types

In two-dimensional image arrays, edges delineate the boundary between patches of significantly different grey levels, while in three-dimensional image arrays, edges mark the boundary between volumetric areas
of different grey levels yielding boundary surfaces (see figure 7.3).

In summary, edges are significant and abrupt changes in the signal
level. In 1D signals, "edges" are zero-dimensional points, in 2D images,
"edges" are one-dimensional lines and in 3D images, "edges" are two-
dimensional surfaces. In the present context, we are primarily interested
in two- and three-dimensional edges. Keep in mind that we will use the
word "edge" for all dimensions.

 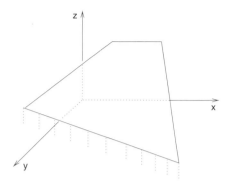

a) an ideal 2D edge   b) an ideal 3D edge plane

Figure 7.3: 2D and 3D Edges

7.2 Simple edge filter masks

Let us now discuss techniques of detecting such edges in digital images using edge filters. Suppose we want to identify picture elements that are likely to be on a boundary that divides two adjacent objects. If these two objects have different average grey values, then we expect such voxels to reflect a significant rate of change of grey values in their immediate neighbourhood.

The rate of change is precisely what is measured by the gradient of an image. Recall that the gradient of a function $f : \mathbb{R}^n \to \mathbb{R}$ is defined as:

$$\nabla f(x_1, ..., x_n) = (\frac{\partial f}{\partial x_1}, ..., \frac{\partial f}{\partial x_n})$$

where

$$\frac{\partial f}{\partial x_i} = \lim_{h \to 0} \frac{f(x_1, ..., x_i, ..., x_n) - f(x_1, ..., x_i + h, ..., x_n)}{h} \tag{7.1}$$

Gradients are useful for enhancing edges in images because they emphasize grey level differences. The greater the difference in the grey level the greater the gradient magnitude will be at this point. In digital images, the gradient cannot be computed directly by the above formula. Instead, we need some discrete approximation. The various edge filters presented in the following section differ in the way in which this approximation is achieved.

Applying a gradient operator to an image amounts to convolving the image with a filter mask that enhances edges. Such filter masks are essentially discrete versions of equation 7.1.

Recall from the previous chapter that convolutions are linear operators defined as:

$$(I * f)(x, y, z) = \int_{-W}^{W} \int_{-W}^{W} \int_{-W}^{W} I(u - x, v - y, w - z) f(u, v, w) du dv dw$$

where $I(x, y, z)$ denotes the image grey value at point (x, y, z), and f denotes the filter function of width W. In the following, we will discuss filter functions f and their discrete analogues that are designed to emphasize grey level differences and to enhance edges.

Perhaps the most elementary way to derive a discrete version of the gradient is to approximate it as a difference of neighbouring grey values. The derivative of a two-dimensional function f can for instance be approximated as:

$$\frac{\partial f(x_1, x_2)}{\partial x_1} \approx \frac{f(x_1 + \Delta x_1, x_2) - f(x_1 - \Delta x_1, x_2)}{2\Delta x_1}$$

and

$$\frac{\partial f(x_1, x_2)}{\partial x_2} \approx \frac{f(x_1, x_2 + \Delta x_2) - f(x_1, x_2 - \Delta x_2)}{2\Delta x_2}$$

This yields two filter masks of the form:

$$\begin{bmatrix} 1 & 1 & 1 \\ 0 & 0 & 0 \\ -1 & -1 & -1 \end{bmatrix} \begin{bmatrix} 1 & 0 & -1 \\ 1 & 0 & -1 \\ 1 & 0 & -1 \end{bmatrix}$$

These filter masks define the so-called *Prewitt operator* [87]. The first mask enhances edges in row orientation, while the second mask enhances edges in column orientation. If p_1 is the filter response from the first mask, and p_2 is the response from the second mask, then the gradient magnitude, which indicates the strength of the edge, is computed as:

$$\sqrt{p_1^2 + p_2^2}.$$

The gradient orientation measured as the angle between the edge and the x-axis, is given by:

$$\arctan\left(\frac{p_1}{p_2}\right).$$

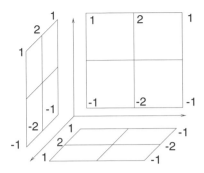

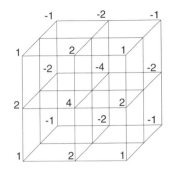

a) Three 18-neighbourhood masks   b) A 26-neighbourhood mask

Figure 7.4: 3D Sobel filter masks

The *2D Sobel operator* is defined much like the Prewitt operator. However, the Sobel operator also smoothes the images in the directions orthogonal to the mask orientations by emphasizing the centre pixel:

$$\begin{bmatrix} 1 & 2 & 1 \\ 0 & 0 & 0 \\ -1 & -2 & -1 \end{bmatrix} \quad \begin{bmatrix} 1 & 0 & -1 \\ 2 & 0 & -2 \\ 1 & 0 & -1 \end{bmatrix}$$

A large number of such filter masks have been developed. We will not go into more detail here. For an excellent overview see [4, p. 337 ff.].

The Generalization to 3D

There are several possible generalizations of the above filter operators to three dimensions. The reason why the generalization is not unique is that we have several different neighbourhood systems, each of which leads to a different 3D version of our operators. For instance, consider the Sobel operator.

For the 18-neighbourhood model, we need three $3 \times 3 \times 1$ masks, each being orthogonal to the others. For the 26-neighbourhood model, we need three $3 \times 3 \times 3$ masks. Note that the central voxels have a heavier weight than the other voxels in the mask. We could even adhere to the 6-neighbourhood model, using three $1 \times 3 \times 1$ masks, each being the central section of the 18-neighbourhood masks. Figure 7.4 shows some of these masks. Remember that we need three masks in each case, one mask for each gradient direction [88].

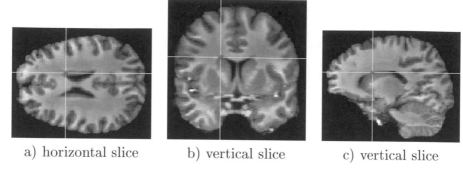

a) horizontal slice   b) vertical slice   c) vertical slice

Figure 7.5: A magnetic resonance image of the human brain

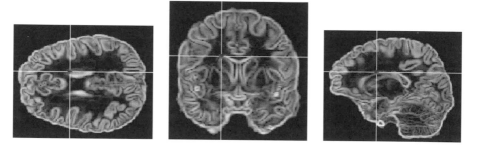

Figure 7.6: Result of a 3D Sobel filtering (cross-sectional slices)

To obtain the gradient magnitude, we must apply a 3D edge filter mask in each of the three principal directions and compute the norm:

$$\parallel \nabla f(x,y,z) \parallel = \sqrt{\frac{\partial f(x,y,z)}{\partial x}^2 + \frac{\partial f(x,y,z)}{\partial y}^2 + \frac{\partial f(x,y,z)}{\partial z}^2}.$$

Note that instead of applying a 3D edge operator to the entire 3D image array, we could also have performed a two-dimensional convolution successively in each slice. However, we would then have failed to detect edges along the slice direction. Figure 7.6 shows the result of a Sobel filter operation applied to a magnetic resonance image of the human brain. The original MR input image is shown in figure 7.5. Both images are displayed as three orthogonal cross-sections through the three-dimensional image volume[1].

---

[1]For more information on this visualization technique see section A.1

Various other filter masks have been proposed for 3D edge detection. Zucker et al. [89] for instance advocated the following mask for determining the gradient response in slice direction. Gradients along the other two directions are defined correspondingly.

$$
\begin{array}{ccc|ccc|ccc}
b & \text{-}a & \text{-}b & 0 & 0 & 0 & b & a & b \\
\text{-}a & \text{-}c & \text{-}a & 0 & 0 & 0 & a & c & a \\
\text{-}b & \text{-}a & \text{-}b & 0 & 0 & 0 & b & a & b
\end{array}
$$

where

$$
a = 1.0, \quad b = \frac{\sqrt{2}}{2}, \quad c = \frac{\sqrt{3}}{3}.
$$

The edge operators we have discussed so far are based on first-order derivatives. Alternatively, one can use second-order derivatives as proposed by Hildreth [90] for two-dimensional images. An extension to the three-dimensional case is described in [91].

7.2.1 The Canny filter

In this section, we will discuss Canny's edge filter [92], which has won great popularity in recent years. In fact, it has become one of the most widely used edge operators, and for that reason, we will present it in more detail. In the following, we will introduce the Canny filter in its one-dimensional, two-dimensional and three-dimensional versions.

First, we look at the one-dimensional case. Suppose we want to detect a step edge in a one-dimensional signal such as the one shown in figure 7.1. To make things easier, we want to use a linear filter $f(x)$ of width W, so that the response to the edge detection is given by the convolution:

$$
F(x) = \int_W^W I(t)f(t - x)dt
$$

where $I(t)$ denotes the input signal.

The problem is now to define a filter function $f(x)$ that will accomplish this task in some "optimal" way. Canny's idea was to formulate the problem of deriving a suitable filter as an optimization problem. We will now present Canny's line of reasoning in an abbreviated form.

The criteria that an optimal filter should fulfil are the following:

1. *Good detection.* Real edges should have a high probability of being detected, while false edges (such as edges due to noise) should have a low probability of being detected.

2. *Good localization.* Points detected by the operator should be close to the real edge.

3. *Only one response to a single edge.* This criterion follows from the first. If too many edges are detected, then obviously some of them must be false edges. However, Canny introduced this third criterion as it turned out to be essential to give it an explicit consideration.

These three criteria can be formalized so that the design of an optimal filter can be cast as an optimization problem. Using variational calculus, it can be shown [92] that the optimal filter derived from the optimization procedure must have the form:

$$f(x) = a_1 \gamma \sin(\omega x) + a_2 \gamma \cos(\omega x) + a_3 \gamma^{-1} \sin(\omega x) + a_4 \gamma^{-1} \cos(\omega x) + C$$
$$(7.2)$$

where $\gamma = e^{\alpha x}$, and α, ω and C are some positive real numbers. The parameters $a_i, i = 1, .., 4$ can be computed from several constraints on the shape of the filter function $f(x)$. First of all remember that we required the filter to be of width W, i.e.

$$f(x) = 0, \text{ if } x > W, \text{ and } f(x) = 0, \text{ if } x < -W.$$

In addition, the filter function must vanish at the point where the edge occurs, and its slope (its derivative) at the edge point must be steep. Also, we want the filter to fade out smoothly at its ends, so that the derivative of f at W also vanishes. In summary, we get the following boundary conditions for f:

$$f(0) = 0, \quad f'(0) = S, \quad f(\pm W) = 0, \quad f'(\pm W) = 0. \qquad (7.3)$$

It can be shown that these boundary conditions sufficiently constrain the choice of the parameters $a_i, i = 1, ..., 4$ to give unique values.

The filter function $f(x)$ defined in 7.2 is quite lengthy and not very well suited for practical applications. Fortunately, there exists an approximation to the function $f(x)$ that is much easier to implement and to handle numerically. This function is the derivative of a Gaussian:

$$f(x) \approx \frac{d}{dx} e^{-x^2/2\sigma^2} = -\frac{x}{\sigma^2} e^{-x^2/2\sigma^2} \qquad (7.4)$$

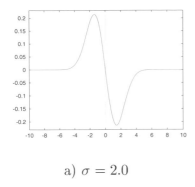
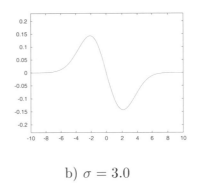

a) $\sigma = 2.0$ b) $\sigma = 3.0$

Figure 7.7: One-dimensional Canny filters

In fact, equation 7.4 is the form that is really used. Figure 7.7 shows this filter function with two values of σ. This filter effectively smoothes the image using a Gaussian function before it computes the derivative of the smoothed image. The parameter σ controls the smoothness. A larger value of σ leads to a greater smoothing effect, which in turn means that the filter is less sensitive to noise. On the other hand, the edge localization is not quite as good.

The two-dimensional Canny filter

As we are primarily interested in two- or three-dimensional data sets, we need to generalize the above considerations. First note that edges in two-dimensional images can no longer be described by a single point, but by a line which divides areas of different grey levels. An edge in such an image also has a direction and not just a magnitude (see figure 7.8).

For simplicity, first suppose that the edge that we want to detect is a straight line of which we know the direction. Then we can simply use the one-dimensional edge detector derived in the previous section. The only thing we have to do in such a case is to do a one-dimensional convolution along the gradient direction using the filter function of equation 7.4.

Unfortunately, life is not so easy, as in general we do not know the gradient direction. However, we can usually obtain a good guess of it by smoothing the image and taking directional derivatives.

Suppose we want to estimate the gradient direction $r(x, y)$ at some point (x, y) in the image. If the image were noise free then we could

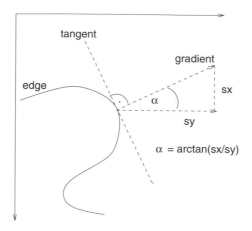

Figure 7.8: The gradient direction

simply estimate $r(x, y)$ by computing the gradient:

$$r(x, y) = \nabla I(x, y).$$

As there usually is noise, we first need to smooth the image by convolving it with a two-dimensional Gaussian $G(x, y)$:

$$G(x, y) = e^{-(x^2+y^2)/2\sigma^2} \tag{7.5}$$

and approximate the gradient direction at (x, y) using the smoothed image:

$$r(x, y) \approx \frac{\nabla(G * I)(x, y)}{\|\nabla(G * I)(x, y)\|}.$$

The term $r(x, y)$ will now be a sufficiently good estimate of the gradient direction at (x, y).

Remember that we can detect the edge in direction $r(x, y)$ by using the one-dimensional Canny filter function, which was the derivative of the Gaussian in direction r. So the filter function we must now use is the directional derivative of the Gaussian, denoted by:

$$G_r = \frac{\partial G}{\partial r}.$$

Edge points show up as local maxima in the gradient image, and so if there is an edge passing through (x, y) in the direction $r(x, y)$ then there will be a local maximum in the image convolved with G_r, so that:

$$\frac{\partial}{\partial r}(G_r * I) = \frac{\partial^2}{\partial^2 r}(G * I) = 0.$$

The gradient magnitude (the "edge strength") at that point will be:

$$\|G_r * I\|.$$

Recall from calculus that the directional derivative of G in the direction r is given by:

$$G_r = \frac{\partial G}{\partial r} = r \cdot \nabla G.$$

And so we can compute the edge strength as:

$$\|G_r * I\| = \|r\| \|\nabla G * I\|.$$

Note that

$$(\nabla G * I) = (\frac{\partial G}{\partial x} * I, \frac{\partial G}{\partial y} * I)$$

and

$$
\begin{aligned}
\frac{\partial G}{\partial x} &= \frac{\partial}{\partial x} e^{-(x^2 + y^2)/2\sigma^2} \\
&= -2x \, e^{-(x^2 + y^2)/2\sigma^2} \\
&= -2x \, e^{-x^2/2\sigma^2} \, e^{-y^2/2\sigma^2} \\
&= \frac{d}{dx} g(x) \, g(y)
\end{aligned}
$$

where $g(t) = e^{-t^2/2\sigma^2}$ is the one-dimensional version of $G(x,y)$.

In other words, we obtain the two-dimensional Canny edge detector as a sequence of two one-dimensional linear filters: we first do a one-dimensional convolution using the derivative of the 1D Gaussian in the first direction (say the row direction), and convolve the resulting image with the one-dimensional Gaussian filter in the orthogonal direction (the column direction).

In the second step, we reverse orders, and do a one-dimensional convolution in the column direction using the derivative of the 1D Gaussian, and smooth the resulting image with the one-dimensional Gaussian filter in the orthogonal direction (the row direction).

The trick that lead to this very elegant form was to use the same standard deviation σ for both the smoothing of the image and for the one-dimensional edge detection filter (see equation 7.5). So to obtain the gradient of a two-dimensional image, we convolve that image in the row direction using the derivative of a Gaussian in that same direction and smooth the result in the orthogonal direction. We proceed likewise in the orthogonal direction. We receive an image having two bands where the first band codes the edge strengths in the row direction and the second band codes the edge strength in the column direction.

The magnitude of the gradient image indicates the edge strength. As before, we compute it using the L_2-Norm:

$$\sqrt{g_x(x,y)^2 + g_y(x,y)^2}.$$

For efficiency reasons, we sometimes use the L_1-Norm instead:

$$|g_x(x,y)| + |g_y(x,y)|$$

where g_x and g_y denote the results of the Canny filter operations in row and column directions, respectively. The direction of the gradient for 2D images is given by (see figure 7.8):

$$\arctan g_x(x,y)/g_y(x,y).$$

The three-dimensional Canny filter

The above line of reasoning carries over to the three-dimensional case without major change. To obtain the x-component of the gradient of a three-dimensional image, we compute a one-dimensional convolution using the derivative of a Gaussian, then we smooth the image by doing two more one-dimensional convolutions, one in the y-direction and the other in the z-direction using a Gaussian filter function. The other components of the gradient are obtained analogously.

As before, we exploit the separability of the Gaussians to reduce the complexity:

$$
\begin{aligned}
\frac{\partial G}{\partial x} &= \frac{\partial}{\partial x} e^{-(x^2+y^2+z^2)/2\sigma^2} \\
&= -2x\ e^{-(x^2+y^2+z^2)/2\sigma^2} \\
&= -2x\ e^{-x^2/2\sigma^2}\ e^{-y^2/2\sigma^2}\ e^{-z^2/2\sigma^2} \\
&= \frac{d}{dx} g(x)\ g(y)\ g(z)
\end{aligned}
$$

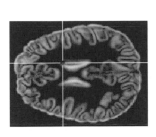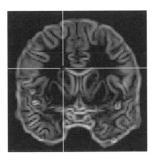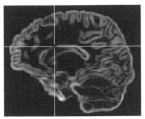

Figure 7.9: Result of 3D Canny filtering (cross-sectional slices)

where $g(t) = e^{-t^2/2\sigma^2}$ is the one-dimensional version of $G(x, y, z)$.

Figure 7.9 shows the result of the 3D Canny filter applied to the magnetic resonance image of figure 7.5. Voxels that have a strong response to the Canny filter are lighter than voxels with a low response. Note that the Canny filter does indeed give a better result than the Sobel filter shown in the previous section. Edges are more clearly localized and less fuzzy.

Implementation issues

The first step towards an implementation is to discretize the mathematics explained above. In particular, we need discrete versions of the analytical filter functions defined in the previous sections.

Let us begin with the discretization of the one-dimensional Gaussian function f:

$$f(x) = \frac{1}{\sqrt{2\pi}\,\sigma}\, e^{-x^2/2\sigma^2}.$$

Figure 7.10 shows plots of this function with various values of σ. To obtain the discrete version of this function, we sample it at integer valued points $i = -n, ..., +n$:

$$f(i) = \frac{1}{\sqrt{2\pi}\,\sigma}\, e^{-i^2/2\sigma^2}.$$

Obviously, the number of points to be sampled depends on the standard deviation σ: the larger the standard deviation, the more points need to be sampled. A good rule of thumb is to use $n = 2\sigma + 1$, so that the filter size is $w = 2n + 1$. For instance, for $\sigma = 1.0$ a filter size of

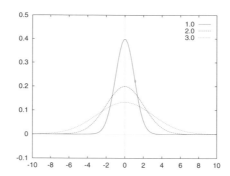

Figure 7.10: The one-dimensional Gaussian with $\sigma = 1.0, \sigma = 2.0, \sigma = 3.0$

$w = 2 \times 3 + 1 = 7$ suffices, while for $\sigma = 2.0$ a window size of $w \times w$ with $w = 2 \times 5 + 1 = 11$ is needed. The first derivative of the Gaussian is sampled analogously.

Occasionally, we may want to approximate the Gaussian to save computation time. The idea is to use Pascal's triangle which gives a very close approximation. The table below lists the values for the first few values of the standard deviation.

	σ^2
1	0
1 1	1/4
1 2 1	1/2
1 3 3 1	3/4
1 4 6 4 1	1
1 5 10 10 5 1	5/4

7.2.2 The Deriche filter

Even though the Canny filter is separable its computational load is still rather heavy. This can become rather tiresome for large 3D data sets. Volumetric data sets often have several hundred rows, columns and slices. For such data, only small filter sizes are feasible.

Fortunately, there exists a method of implementing a variation of Canny's filter in a much faster, recursive fashion. This method is the *Deriche Filter* [93], [94] which we will present in the following.

As before, we start by analysing the one-dimensional case. Deriche used essentially the same line of reasoning as Canny with one exception.

While Canny sought an optimal filter of finite width W, Deriche derived an optimal filter of infinite width using the same optimality criteria as Canny.

The result of the optimization process is a one-dimensional filter function of the form:

$$f(x) = -c\,e^{-\alpha|x|}\sin(\omega x)$$

with the boundary conditions:

$$f(0) = 0, \quad f(+\infty) = 0 \quad f'(0) = S, \quad f'(+\infty) = 0.$$

As with the Canny filter there also exists a simplified version of this function:

$$\sin(\omega x) \approx \omega x,$$

so that:

$$f(x) = -c\,x\,e^{-\alpha|x|}.$$

Surprisingly, this function can be implemented very efficiently as follows. Let g^+ and g^- denote two one-dimensional arrays. For the moment, one may think of these arrays as representing one image row. To compute the 1D gradient along one row using Deriche's approach, we recursively fill values into these arrays as follows:

$$g^+(m) = x(m-1) - b_1 g^+(m-1) + b_2 g^+(m-2), \qquad (7.6)$$

$$g^-(m) = x(m+1) - b_1 g^-(m+1) + b_2 g^-(m+2), \qquad (7.7)$$

$$g(m) = -ce^{-\alpha}\,(g^+(m) + g^-(m))$$

with

$$b_1 = -2e^{-\alpha} \text{ and } b_2 = e^{-2\alpha}.$$

The derivation of this recursive form is given in [93]. The important point here is that the computational load of the Deriche filter is much smaller than that of the Canny filter, although Deriche's filter is an infinite response filter. In fact, the computation time is independent of the size of the smoothing parameter α. Even a large α does not require more arithmetic operations. The Canny filter, on the other hand, requires a larger convolution kernel for large values of *sigma*. This fact makes the Deriche filter particularly attractive for three-dimensional images.

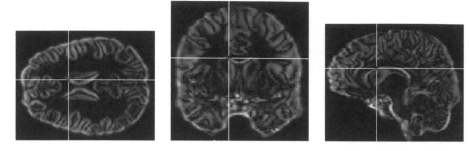

Figure 7.11: Result of a slice-by-slice 2D Deriche filtering

The 3-dimensional Deriche filter

Using the same line of reasoning as for the Canny filter, we can now extend Deriche's filter to the three-dimensional case. As before, the three components of the gradient are computed by first applying the filter function in one direction and smoothing the image in the other two orthogonal directions. The only difference is that we use a different type of smoothing function this time. Remember that in Canny's case, the smoothing filter function was really the integral of the edge filter function.

So we need to compute the integral of our new edge filter function f, which turns out to be:

$$l(t) = s\left(\alpha * |t| + 1\right) e^{(-\alpha|t|)}.$$

Using an argumentation similar to the one for the edge filter function, we can also derive a recursive version of the smoothing filter function, which we will not present here (for details see [93], [94]). The recursive form of the smoothing filter function is:

$$f^+(m) = a_0 v(m) + a_1 v(m-1) - b_1 f^+(m-1) - b_2 f^+(m-2),$$

$$f^-(m) = a_2 v(m+1) + a_3 v(m+2) - b_1 f^-(m+1) - b_2 f^-(m+2),$$

$$f(m) = (f^+(m) + f^-(m)) \text{ for } m = 1, ..., M,$$

where $v(m)$ denotes the grey value at the current location in the input image and

$$a_0 = \frac{(1 - e^{-\alpha})^2}{1 + 2\alpha e^{-\alpha} - e^{-2\alpha}}$$

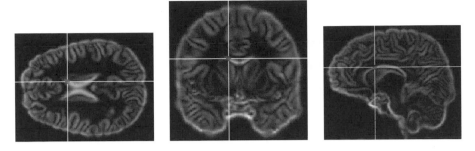

Figure 7.12: Result of a 3D Deriche filtering

$$a_1 = a_0(\alpha - 1)e^{-\alpha}, \ a_2 = a_1 - a_0 b_1, \ a_3 = -a_0 b_2$$

and

$$b_1 = -2e^{-\alpha}, \ b_2 = e^{-2\alpha}.$$

Remember that in order to compute a partial derivative using Deriche's aproach, we must compute three one-dimensional recursive filters: one yielding the derivative and the two others performing the smoothing in the two directions orthogonal to the derivative direction [95]. For instance, to compute the partial derivative in the column direction we must apply the following three recursive filters in sequence:

$$
\begin{aligned}
g^+(c) &= v(b, r, c - 1) - b_1 g^+(c - 1) + b_2 g^+(c - 2) \\
g^-(c) &= v(b, r, c + 1) - b_1 g^-(c + 1) + b_2 g^-(c + 2) \\
g(c) &= e^{-\alpha} \left(g^+(c) + g^-(c) \right), \text{ for } c = 0, 1, ..., n_c
\end{aligned}
$$

$$
\begin{aligned}
f^+(r) &= a_0 g(b, r, c) + a_1 g(b, r - 1, c) - b_1 f^+(r - 1) - b_2 f^+(r - 2) \\
f^-(r) &= a_2 g(b, r + 1, c) + a_3 g(b, r + 2, c) - b_1 f^-(r + 1) - b_2 f^-(r + 2) \\
f(r) &= \left(f^+(r) + f^-(r) \right), \text{ for } r = 0, 1, ..., n_r
\end{aligned}
$$

$$
\begin{aligned}
h^+(b) &= a_0 f(b, r, c) + a_1 f(b - 1, r, c) - b_1 h^+(b - 1) - b_2 h^+(b - 2) \\
h^-(b) &= a_2 f(b + 1, r, c) + a_3 f(b + 2, r, c) - b_1 h^-(b + 1) - b_2 h^-(b + 2) \\
h(b) &= \left(h^+(b) + h^-(b) \right), \text{ for } b = 0, 1, ..., n_b.
\end{aligned}
$$

```
VImage
ColGradient(VImage src,double alpha)
{
    double left[NUMCOLS],right[NUMCOLS];

    a = 1.0 * exp(- alpha);
    b1 = -2.0 * exp(- alpha);
    b2 = exp(-2.0 * alpha);

    for (b=0; b<nbands; b++) {
        for (r=0; r<nrows; r++) {
            left[0] = 0; /* left-to-right direction */
            left[1] = 0;
            for (c=2; c<ncols; c++) {
                left[c] = VGetPixel(src,b,r,c-1)
                    - b1 * left[c-1] - b2 * left[c-2];
            }
            right[ncols-1] = 0; /* right-to-left direction */
            right[ncols-2] = 0;
            for (c=ncols-3; c>=0; c--) {
                right[c] = VGetPixel(src,b,r,c+1)
                    - b1 * right[c+1] - b2 * right[c+2];
            }
            for (c=0; c<ncols; c++) { /* combine */
                VSetPixel(dest,b,r,c) = a * (left[c] - right[c]);
            }
        }
    }
    return dest;
}
```

Figure 7.13: Deriche edge detection

Figure 7.12 shows the result of a 3D Deriche filtering applied to our previous magnetic resonance image. For comparison, a slice-by-slice 2D Deriche filter was applied to the same image (figure 7.11). The left images show the horizontal slices, while the two right images show the two vertical cross-sections. As you can see quite clearly, the slice-by-slice method performs poorly in detecting vertical edges although it detects horizontal edges quite well.

In figure 7.13 a small portion of the C-code for computing one of these nine one-dimensional recursive filters is given. This particular one computes the derivative along the column direction. The smoothing along the slice- and row directions must follow to yield the complete approximation to the partial derivative in the column direction.

7.3 Edge thinning

The edge filters introduced in the previous sections give us a set of voxels that are good candidates for being on an object surface. However, most of the time we will have far too many candidate voxels. Look again at figure 7.12. Clearly, there are many voxels that group around the true edge.

In this section, we will introduce methods of extracting a thin one-voxel thick layer of edge voxels. These methods are called "edge thinning". By doing edge thinning we remove surplus voxels from our list of candidate edge voxels.

The principal idea underlying edge thinning is the following. Consider a line passing through a voxel at location (x, y, z) in the direction of the gradient. If this voxel is located on an edge, then its gradient magnitude must be a local maximum along that line. If it is not a maximum, then we no longer consider it a candidate edge voxel, and we "suppress" it. If it is a maximum, then we retain it. "Suppressing" a voxel means that we set its values to zero, and "retaining" a voxel means that we leave its value unchanged.

In summary, the basic steps in edge thinning are the following:

1. inspect a line through each voxel along its gradient direction,

2. if the voxel is a local maximum along that line, retain the voxel, else suppress it.

The difficult part now is to identify voxels that are located along the line in the gradient direction. Remember that we obtained the gradient direction from the edge filtering described in the previous sections. However, the gradient direction will most often not point exactly to an adjacent voxel, but rather it will point anywhere between several adjacent voxels.

There are various approaches to deal with this problem. In the following, we will present two methods of edge thinning, which differ in the way in which they identify voxels along the gradient direction.

7.3.1 Non-maxima suppression using masks

The first method employs filter masks to identify voxels along the gradient direction.

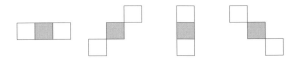

Figure 7.14: The 2D masks for non-maxima suppression

Let us first consider the 2D case. In 2D, we need to find two adjacent pixels of our current pixel along the gradient direction. If for instance the gradient direction is roughly horizontal, then we inspect the two horizontally adjacent neighbours to see whether their gradient magnitude is smaller than the current pixel's gradient magnitude. If it is, we leave the current pixel unchanged, otherwise we set its value to zero. Likewise, we proceed with the other gradient directions. In the 2D case, it is customary to distinguish between four different gradient directions: "horizontal" ,"vertical", "left-diagonal" and "right-diagonal". Below is a list of these directions together with the angles that specify them.

horizontal: $333.7^o \leq \theta \leq 22.5^o$ and $157.5^o \leq \theta \leq 202.5^o$
vertical: $67.5^o \leq \theta \leq 112.5^o$ and $247.5^o \leq \theta \leq 337.5^o$
diagonal: $22.5^o \leq \theta \leq 67.5^o$ and $202.5^o \leq \theta \leq 247.5^o$
diagonal: $112.5^o \leq \theta \leq 157.5^o$ and $292.5^o \leq \theta \leq 337.5^o$

Here are the steps of our 2D edge thinning algorithm:

- for each pixel:

  1. compute the gradient direction α of the current pixel.

  2. select a mask from the above list such that α is orthogonal to the mask direction θ, i.e. $\theta = \alpha + 90^o$ or $\theta = \alpha + 270^o$.

  3. inspect the gradient directions of the two pixels covered by the selected mask. If their directions differs "too much" (say more than 90°) from the gradient direction of the current pixel then they are probably not on the same edge. So we cannot use them for thinning the edge of the current pixel.

  4. Otherwise, the two adjacent pixels do belong to the same edge as the current pixel. If the gradient magnitude of the current pixel is larger than the gradient magnitude of both neighbouring pixels, then retain its value, else set it to zero.

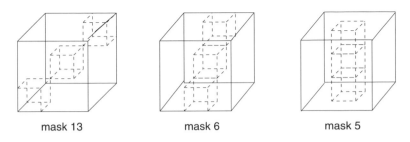

mask 13   mask 6   mask 5

Figure 7.15: Some 3D masks used for non-maxima suppression

3D non-maxima suppression using masks

The edge thinning algorithm defined above for 2D images easily carries over to the 3D case. We only need to adapt the masks used for identifying the adjacent pixels along the gradient direction. In 3D images, there are many more neighbouring voxels that we must consider.

In the 2D case, we needed to inspect eight neighbours of each pixel, which were covered by half as many masks. In 3D, there are 26 neighbours and consequently 13 masks that we need to consider. A list of all 13 masks is given below. Some of these masks are also shown in figure 7.15.

mask	coordinates of 1st neighbour	coordinates of 2nd neighbour
1	$(z, y, x-1)$	$(z, y, x+1)$
2	$(z-1, y, x)$	$(z+1, y, x)$
3	$(z+1, y, x+1)$	$(z-1, y, x-1)$
4	$(z-1, y, x+1)$	$(z+1, y, x-1)$
5	$(z, y+1, x)$	$(z, y-1, x)$
6	$(z-1, y+1, x)$	$(z+1, y-1, z)$
7	$(z-1, y-1, x)$	$(z+1, y+1, x)$
8	$(z, y-1, x-1)$	$(z, y+1, x+1)$
9	$(z, y+1, x-1)$	$(z, y-1, x-1)$
10	$(z-1, y-1, x+1)$	$(z+1, y+1, x-1)$
11	$(z+1, y+1, x+1)$	$(z-1, y-1, x-1)$
12	$(z+1, y-1, x-1)$	$(z-1, y+1, x+1)$
13	$(z+1, y-1, x+1)$	$(z-1, y+1, x-1)$

Figures 7.16 illustrates the effect of edge thinning. Note that the thinned images appear be less smooth after thinning. This effect is due to the "erosion" incurred by the thinning process.

 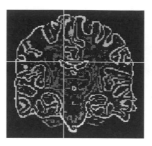 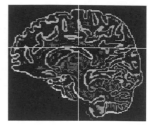

Figure 7.16: The effect of edge thinning

7.3.2　Non-maxima suppression using interpolation

In this section, we will present another method of non-maxima suppression based on gradient interpolation. This method generally gives more accurate results but it is also slower. The general idea is to estimate the gradient magnitude in the vicinity of the current pixel by interpolating the gradient magnitudes of neighbouring pixels. As before, the current pixel is suppressed if its gradient magnitude is small compared with the gradient magnitude computed in its vicinity. We begin by presenting the 2D case.

Non-maxima suppression in 2D using gradient interpolation

Consider a line passing through the current pixel P along the direction of the gradient computed at P (see also figure 7.17). This line intersects the square spanned by the eight neighbouring pixels of P in exactly two points, which we call S_1 and S_2. We now estimate the gradient magnitude at those two points. If the gradient magnitude at P is less than the gradient at either S_1 or S_2 or both, then we suppress P, otherwise we retain its value.

The important part now is to estimate the gradient magnitude at S_1 and S_2. Consider the two pixels adjacent to S_1. Let us call them P_1 and P_2, and let d denote the distance between P_1 and S_1. We can then obtain a realistic estimate of the gradient magnitude at S_1 by averaging the gradient magnitudes at P_1 and P_2 as follows:

$$G_{S_1} \approx (1-d)\,G_1 + d\,G_2$$

where G_i denotes the gradient magnitude at $P_i, i = 1, 2$. Remember

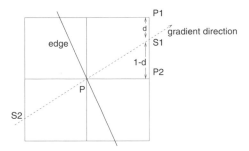

Figure 7.17: 2D gradient interpolation

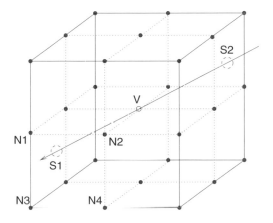

Figure 7.18: 3D gradient interpolation

that we know estimates of these magnitudes from the edge filtering defined in section 7.2.1.

Non-maxima suppression in 3D using gradient interpolation

The 3D case is now quite similar. However, the current voxel is now surrounded by a cube spanned by its 26-adjacent voxels, where the line passing through the gradient direction intersects two faces of this cube (see figure 7.18). Note that this cube has 24 faces, and the vertices of each face are the adjacent voxels. Let us denote the two points where the gradient line hits those two faces as S_1 and S_2. And let $N_i, i = 1, ..., 4$ denote the four voxels that form the vertices of the face penetrated at S_1. Again, we want to estimate the gradient strength at S_1 and S_2. Of course, we need a slightly different interpolating formula

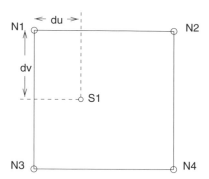

Figure 7.19: The interpolating formula

now. In fact, several different interpolating formulas are conceivable here. We suggest the following (see figure 7.19):

$$G_{S_1} \approx (1 - d_u)(1 - d_v)G_1 + d_u(1 - d_v)G_2 + d_u d_v G_3 + (1 - d_u)d_v G_4$$

where d_u denotes the distance between the x-components of S_1 and N_1, d_v denotes the distance between the y-components of S_1 and N_1 and $G_i, i = 1, .., 4$ denote the gradient magnitude at voxels $N_i, i = 1, \ldots, 4$. This formula has several advantageous properties: first of all, if S_1 is located in the centre of the face, then all four voxels at the face's vertices contribute to the G_{S_1} by the same amount. Secondly, if S_1 is located somewhere on the perimeter of the face, then only the two neighbouring vertices contribute to G_{S_1}. Thirdly, G_{S_1} is influenced most strongly by the vertices closest to it.

7.4   Edge linking

The result of the edge thinning is a one-voxel thick layer of voxels that probably delineate object boundaries. However, as you can see from figure 7.16 there are still a lot of voxels which most likely are due to noise or which belong to very weak edges. Clearly, we would like to remove these voxels so that only true edge voxels remain. In addition, we would also like to make explicit which voxels are adjacent or belong to the same edge surface. This is the goal of *edge linking*. Figure 7.20 shows the result of such an operation applied to a portion of the image shown in figure 7.16.

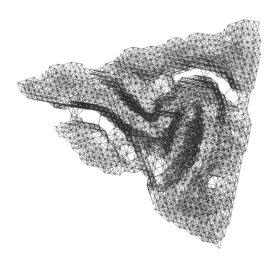

Figure 7.20: Edge linking

To get rid of voxels having low gradient values we could simply threshold the result of the edge thinning procedure so that only voxels above a certain minimal gradient magnitude remain. However, this approach usually leads to unsatisfactory results as the gradient magnitude varies a lot even within a single edge.

A way around this problem is given by a technique called *hysteresis thresholding*. The basic idea [95], [92] of hysteresis thresholding is the following. We begin by listing a set of criteria that describe valid edge points:

- the gradient magnitude of each edge point must be larger than some minimal threshold t_{low},

- each edge point must be linked into a 26-connected component of a certain minimal size s_{min},

- each such connected component must have at least one edge point whose gradient magnitude is larger than a threshold t_{high}.

The algorithm proceeds in three stages. We begin by classifying all candidate edge points into three classes depending on their gradient magnitude as follows. We assemble all candidate edge points into a list in which we ignore all those points whose gradient magnitude falls below the threshold t_{low}.

- if $\| \nabla g(b, r, c) \| < t_{low}$, then ignore the point at (b, r, c).

- if $t_{low} \leq \| \nabla g(b, r, c) \| < t_{high}$, then insert the 4-tuple (b, r, c, t_{low}) into the list.

- if $\| \nabla g(b, r, c) \| \geq t_{high}$, then insert the 4-tuple (b, r, c, t_{high}) into the list.

At the end of this stage, the list contains candidate edge points, where points that certainly belong to an edge are marked by the label t_{high} and points of which we are not yet sure are marked by the label t_{low}.

During the second stage of the procedure, we assemble edge points into connected components. We can now use a depth first search approach similar to the one introduced in the first chapter.

Remember that each connected component must have at least one point marked t_{high}. Therefore, we start out with any arbitrary point marked t_{high} in this list, remove it from the list and insert it into the first edge set. We then investigate its 26-neighbourhood. If there are any 26-adjacent candidate edge points they are also inserted into the first edge set and removed from the list.

We proceed in a recursive fashion until no unvisited points adjacent to any of the points in this first edge set are found. As we assemble points into this set, we increment a counter that counts the number of its elements. After the first edge set is complete, we decide on whether the entire edge set should be retained or not depending on the number of its elements. If it contains fewer than s_{min} elements it is discarded.

This entire process is repeated until all points have either been removed from the list (because they have been processed) or are marked as t_{low} and are not adjacent to any of the points in the newly formed edge sets. Figure 7.21 shows the result of edge linking applied to the image of figure 7.16. Note that small and weak edges have been removed.

Some improvements in this procedure are conceivable. First of all, the process of assembling connected components can become quite slow as at each step the entire list may have to be searched to detect the

 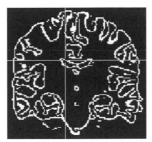 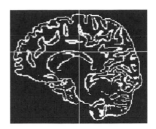

Figure 7.21: Hysteresis thresholding

26-neighbours of a point. To speed up this process, the list may for instance be organized as a hash table, which would allow faster access to the 26-neighbours of an element.

Secondly, a smoothness constraint can be imposed to suppress spurious peaks in the edge surface that may be attributable to noise. Monga et al. [95] suggest suppressing edge points that deviate too much from the tangent plane of adjacent points.

In addition, we may want to close small holes in the surface. This can for instance be achieved by applying a morphological closing filter as described in section 4.5. Edge thinning can sometimes also be achieved by applying a skeletonization as described in section 4.2. However, while this method works quite well for two-dimensional images, it often fails for volumetric images.

7.5 Curvature

In the previous section, we discussed methods of extracting surfaces from 3D images. We will now introduce methods of computing features of those surfaces. Most importantly, we will talk about curvature properties at surface points. We will begin by reviewing material from differential geometry needed to define curvature before discussing algorithms for curvature computation.

7.5.1 Mathematical background

In this section, we will review some of the mathematical background on curvature. For more detail see [96]. Let us first look at planar curves defined in the two-dimensional continuous space $\mathbb{R}^2$. Let $g(t) \in \mathbb{R}^2$

Figure 7.22: A planar curve

be a curve given parametrically in terms of an arc length parameter t
so that the points on the curve are determined by the set

$$C = \{g(t) \in \mathbb{R}^2 \mid t \in \mathbb{R}\}.$$

Figure 7.22 shows an example of such a curve.

Curvature in points along such curves can be expressed in terms of
their normals. Note that at points along the curve where the curvature
is high the rate of change in the direction into which the normals point
is also high, whereas at low curvature points the reverse is true. In
addition, the directions of the normals give information about convexity
or concavity. At convex regions the directions of the normals diverge
and at concavities they converge. Thus, the directions of the normals
and their rate of change is indicative of curvature properties. In fact,
from differential geometry we know that the curvature K at a point p
on a curve is given by the quantity:

$$K = \frac{g''(t)}{(1 + g'(t)^2)^{3/2}}. \tag{7.8}$$

Curvatures on surfaces are more difficult to define as there are in-
finitely many curves through a point. Therefore, we cannot directly
generalize the definition of curvature of planar curves to curvature of
points on a surface. However, we an identify at least one direction in
which the curvature is maximal and some other direction of minimal
curvature. Figure 7.23 illustrates this point. These two directions are
generally called the *principal directions* and are denoted as

$$t_1 \text{ and } t_2.$$

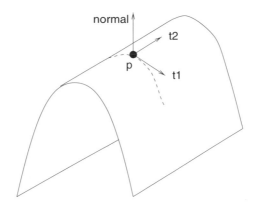

Figure 7.23: Principal curvature directions

Given the principal directions, we can identify a curve through point p along those directions and employ equation 7.8 to compute the curvature along these curves. The magnitude of the curvature along the t_1 and t_2 directions are usually denoted as

$$k_1 \text{ and } k_2.$$

Note that sometimes – for instance for entirely flat surfaces – more than two principal directions exist. In this case, we can use any arbitrary curve of maximal or minimal curvature to compute $t_i, k_i, i = 1, 2$.

The two principal curvatures give rise to the following definitions of curvature on surfaces. Let k_1, k_2 be the principal curvatures at some point p on the surface. Then the term

$$K = k_1 k_2 \tag{7.9}$$

is called the *Gaussian curvature*. The term

$$H = (k_1 + k_2)/2 \tag{7.10}$$

is called the *mean curvature*.

Both types of curvature locally determine the shape of the surface around point p. Figure 7.24 illustrates some curvature types. Note that the surface is locally elliptic if the Gaussian curvature is positive and it is hyperbolic – or formed like a saddle – if it is negative. The mean curvature determines whether the surface is locally convex or concave. If both K and H equal zero then the surface is flat.

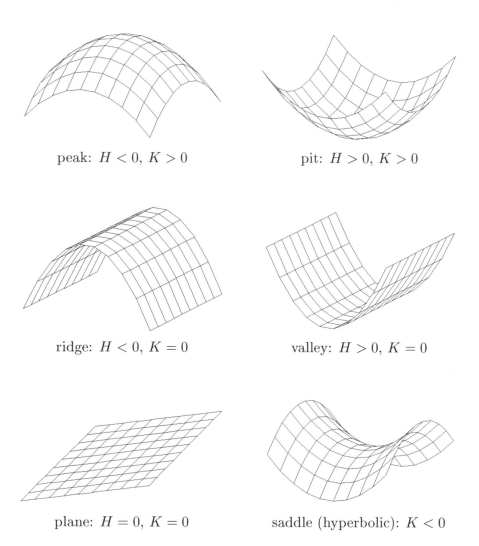

peak: $H < 0$, $K > 0$ pit: $H > 0$, $K > 0$

ridge: $H < 0$, $K = 0$ valley: $H > 0$, $K = 0$

plane: $H = 0$, $K = 0$ saddle (hyperbolic): $K < 0$

Figure 7.24: Curvature classes

7.5.2 Curvature computation

Clearly, the above definitions of curvature are not well suited to practical computation as it would be quite tedious to search for the principal curvature directions. Fortunately, there exist alternative ways for computing curvatures, which we will now present without proof. For more

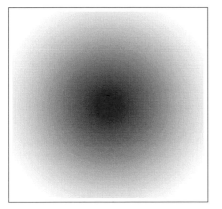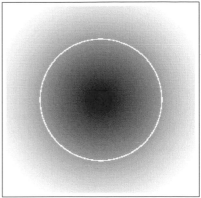

Figure 7.25: Iso-contours

detail see for instance [96], [97], [98], [99].

Curvature is a local property attached to points on a surface. Let us therefore first define surface points. Let $f(x, y, z)$ denote the grey values of a 3D image. For the moment we assume that the image is continuous, so that $(x, y, z) \in \mathbb{R}^3$. The *iso-surface* I_a at level a is defined as the set of points defined by:

$$I_a = \{(x, y, z) \in \mathbb{R}^3 \mid f(x, y, z) = a\}.$$

For instance, suppose an image showing a bell-shaped distribution of grey values is given as illustrated in figure 7.25. Then the iso-surfaces form ellipsoids around the bell's centre with various radii. We are interested in iso-surfaces because we assume that they delineate boundaries between objects.

If the object depicted in the image has some patches of constant grey values, then the iso-surface will not really be a surface but a volume. Without loss of generality we may assume that such a case does not occur. In cases where such problems do occur, we simply modify the boundary by giving it some intermediate value and proceed from there.

Let

$$S = \{(x, y, z) \mid f(x, y, z) = a\}$$

denote the iso-surface at level a. Then at each point $p = (x, y, z)$ on the surface there exists some neighbourhood U of p in which the iso-surface can be expressed by some function $\phi(u, v)$ such that

$$(x = u, y = v, y = \phi(u, v)) \quad \text{and} \quad f(u, v, \phi(u, v)) = a.$$

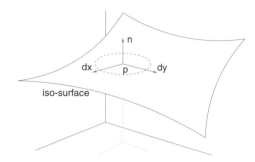

Figure 7.26: Surface normals

Thus, the function ϕ provides a *local* parameterization of the surface in terms of the new parameters (u, v). Figure 7.26 illustrates this fact.

Remember that first and second derivatives were needed to define curvature along planar curves. Analogously, we need first and second partial derivatives defined in U to describe curvature properties within U:

$$\frac{\partial f(u,v)}{\partial u}, \quad \frac{\partial f(u,v)}{\partial v}, \quad \frac{\partial f^2(u,v)}{\partial u \partial v}, \quad \frac{\partial f^2(u,v)}{\partial u^2}, \quad \frac{\partial f^2(u,v)}{\partial v^2}. \quad (7.11)$$

Let $f(u, v, \phi(u, v,))$ denote the locally parameterized surface patch U. From differential geometry [96], we know that Gaussian and mean curvature can be alternatively defined in terms of the following first- and second-order partial derivatives of f using the new parameters u and v as follows:

$$E = \frac{\partial S}{\partial u} \cdot \frac{\partial S}{\partial u} \quad (7.12)$$

$$F = \frac{\partial S}{\partial u} \cdot \frac{\partial S}{\partial v} \quad (7.13)$$

$$G = \frac{\partial S}{\partial v} \cdot \frac{\partial S}{\partial v} \quad (7.14)$$

$$L = \frac{\partial^2 S}{\partial u^2} \cdot Q \quad (7.15)$$

$$M = \frac{\partial^2 S}{\partial u \partial v} \cdot Q \quad (7.16)$$

$$N = \frac{\partial^2 S}{\partial v^2} \cdot Q \qquad (7.17)$$

where

$$Q = \frac{\frac{\partial S}{\partial u} \times \frac{\partial S}{\partial v}}{\| \frac{\partial S}{\partial u} \times \frac{\partial S}{\partial v} \|}$$

Given the above quantities, we can formulate a new definition of Gaussian and mean curvature as follows:

$$K = \det \begin{bmatrix} E & F \\ F & G \end{bmatrix}^{-1} \begin{bmatrix} E & F \\ F & G \end{bmatrix} = \frac{LN - M^2}{EG - F^2} \qquad (7.18)$$

$$H = \frac{1}{2} \operatorname{trace} \begin{bmatrix} E & F \\ F & G \end{bmatrix}^{-1} \begin{bmatrix} L & M \\ M & N \end{bmatrix} = \frac{EN - 2FM + GL}{2\left(EG - F^2\right)} \qquad (7.19)$$

These definitions are in fact equivalent to our previous definition given by equations 7.9 and 7.10. The problem of curvature computation now consists in finding the partial derivatives of equation 7.17. Sander et al.[100], [101] suggest the following approach. They begin by computing local quadratic surface patches at each surface point such that the parameterized surface is given by:

$$S(u, v) = (u, v, \phi(u, v)) = (u, v, au^2 + 2buv + cv^2).$$

As it is quite easy to compute second-order partial derivatives on such surface patches, the problem of computing partial derivatives thus reduces to determining the parameters a, b, c that describe the surface patch. This can be usually achieved by some optimization technique. While this method works quite well for smooth surfaces, problems may arise if the surface is folded too strongly. In those cases, it may not be possible to find a suitable surface patch around a surface point which is large enough to permit the computation of derivatives.

Alternatively, one may directly compute the partial derivatives from the raster image without the use of continuous surface patches, as proposed by Thirion et al. [97]. We will now present this approach in some more detail. Let us use the following abbreviations for denoting partial derivatives:

$$f_x = \frac{\partial f}{\partial x}, \ f_y = \frac{\partial f}{\partial y}, \ f_z = \frac{\partial f}{\partial z},$$

$$f_{xx} = \frac{\partial^2 f}{\partial x^2}, \ f_{yy} = \frac{\partial^2 f}{\partial y^2}, \ f_{zz} = \frac{\partial^2 f}{\partial z^2},$$

$$f_{xy} = \frac{\partial^2 f}{\partial xy}, \ f_{xz} = \frac{\partial^2 f}{\partial xz}, \ f_{yz} = \frac{\partial^2 f}{\partial yz}.$$

As the surface is given by an implicit equation as

$$S(u, v) \ = \ (u, v, \phi(u, v)) \ = \ a$$

for some iso-value a where $(u = x, \ v = y, \ z = \phi(u, v))$ we may use implicit differentiation and the chain rule to obtain the partial derivatives with respect to x, y and z:

$$\frac{\partial \phi}{\partial u} \ = \ -\frac{f_x}{f_z}, \tag{7.20}$$

$$\frac{\partial \phi}{\partial v} \ = \ -\frac{f_y}{f_z}, \tag{7.21}$$

$$\frac{\partial^2 \phi}{\partial u^2} \ = \ \frac{2 f_x f_z f_{xz} - f_x^2 f_{zz} - f_z^2 f_{xx}}{f_z^3} \tag{7.22}$$

$$\frac{\partial^2 \phi}{\partial v^2} \ = \ \frac{2 f_y f_z f_{yz} - f_y^2 f_{zz} - f_z^2 f_{yy}}{f_z^3} \tag{7.23}$$

$$\frac{\partial^2 \phi}{\partial u \partial v} \ = \ \frac{f_{xz} f_y f_z + f_{yz} f_x f_z - f_{zz} f_x f_y - f_z^2 f_{xy}}{f_z^3} \tag{7.24}$$

Inserting these terms into equations 7.18 and 7.19 yields:

$$E \ = \ \frac{\partial S(u, v)}{\partial u} \cdot \frac{\partial S(u, v)}{\partial u} \ = \ (1, 0, -\frac{f_x}{f_z}) \cdot (1, 0, -\frac{f_x}{f_z}) = 1 + \frac{f_x^2}{f_z^2}$$

$$F \ = \ \frac{\partial S(u, v)}{\partial u} \cdot \frac{\partial S(u, v)}{\partial v} \ = \ (1, 0, -\frac{f_y}{f_z}) \cdot (0, 1, -\frac{f_y}{f_z}) = 1 + \frac{f_x f_y}{f_z^2}$$

$$G \ = \ \frac{\partial S(u, v)}{\partial v} \cdot \frac{\partial S(u, v)}{\partial v} \ = \ (0, 1, -\frac{f_y}{f_z}) \cdot (0, 1, -\frac{f_y}{f_z}) = 1 + \frac{f_y^2}{f_z^2}$$

where " · " denotes the scalar product. The remaining second-order partials can be computed analogously:

$$\begin{aligned}
L \ &= \ (2 f_x f_z f_{xz} - f_x^2 f_{zz} - f_z^2 f_{xx}) \ / \ R \\
M \ &= \ (f_x f_z f_{yz} + f_y f_z f_{xz} - f_x f_y f_{zz} - f_z^2 f_{xy}) \ / \ R \\
N \ &= \ (2 f_y f_z f_{yz} - f_y^2 f_{zz} - f_z^2 f_{yy}) \ / \ R
\end{aligned}$$

where

$$R = f_z^3 \sqrt{\frac{f_x^2 + f_y^2 + f_z^2}{f_z^2}}$$

Note that these terms are not symmetric with respect to the coordinate axis. In fact, they are not even defined if f_z equals zero. From this fact one might be deceived into believing that our previous definitions of curvature might also not be symmetric with respect to the coordinate axis and therefore not rotationally invariant.

Fortunately however, this is not the case as can be seen by inserting the above terms into formulas 7.18, 7.19. Rearranging terms and some algebra yields a new formulation of our curvature definition which is free of any such problems.

$$K = \frac{1}{h^2}[\quad f_x^2 \ (f_{yy}f_{zz} - f_{yz}^2) + 2f_y f_z(f_{xz}f_{xy} - f_{xx}f_{yx}) +$$
$$f_y^2 \ (f_{xx}f_{zz} - f_{xz}^2) + 2f_x f_z(f_{yz}f_{xy} - f_{yy}f_{xz}) +$$
$$f_z^2 \ (f_{xx}f_{yy} - f_{xy}^2) + 2f_x f_y(f_{xz}f_{yz} - f_{zz}f_{xy})]$$

$$H = \frac{1}{2h^{3/2}}[\quad f_x^2 \ (f_{yy} + f_{zz}) - 2f_y f_z f_{yz} +$$
$$f_y^2 \ (f_{xx} + f_{zz}) - 2f_x f_z f_{xz} +$$
$$f_z^2 \ (f_{xx} + f_{yy}) - 2f_x f_y f_{xy} \ ]$$

where $h = f_x^2 + f_y^2 + f_z^2$.

Once the values for H and K are determined, we can easily compute the two principal curvatures using the following equation:

$$k_i = H \pm \sqrt{H^2 - K}, \ i = 1, 2 \qquad (7.25)$$

The corresponding principal directions are given by the eigenvectors of the matrix in equation 7.18.

Computing second-order derivatives

Recall from section 7.2.1 that first-order derivatives can be computed by convolving the image with the derivative of a Gaussian in one direction and smoothing it with Gaussians of the same standard deviation in the

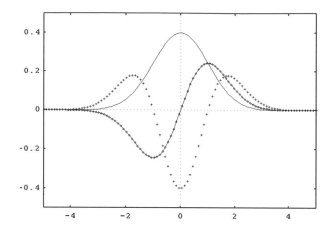

Figure 7.27: A Gaussian and its 1st and 2nd derivatives

two orthogonal directions. In the following, we will generalize this idea
to obtain higher-order differentials.

First note that curvature only needs to be computed on those voxels which belong to the iso-surface, which generally make up only a
small percentage of the total number of voxels in the image. However,
performing three separate one-dimensional convolutions as in Canny
filtering requires us to process the entire image three times. While this
computationally advantageous if measurements must be made at each
voxel location, it is quite inefficient if only a few voxels need to be
processed.

In addition, we need to compute nine different types of first- and
second-order derivatives, which would require us to store nine gradient
images if we were to use one-dimensional filter masks. For both reasons,
we use three-dimensional filter masks to compute the derivatives locally
as they are needed. They can be obtained from the one-dimensional
masks as follows.

Let $g(t)$ denote a one-dimensional Gaussian function, and $g'(t), g''(t)$
its first and second derivatives, as given below:

$$
\begin{aligned}
g(t) &= c\, e^{-t^2/2\sigma^2} \\
g'(t) &= -\frac{tc}{\sigma^2}\, e^{-t^2/2\sigma^2}
\end{aligned}
$$

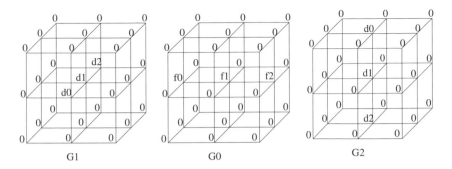

Figure 7.28: Directional filter masks

$$g''(t) \quad = \quad \frac{c}{\sigma^2}\, e^{-t^2/2\sigma^2} \left(\frac{t^2}{\sigma^2} - 1 \right)$$

where $c = 1/(\sigma\sqrt{2\pi})$.

Let G_0 denote a three-dimensional filter mask of size $n \times n \times n$ corresponding to $g(t)$ emulating a one-dimensional convolution. Then $G_0(x)$ contains mostly zeros except in places along a line leading in the x-direction through the mask centre where the discretized values of $g(t)$ are stored. Likewise, G_1, G_2 denote the filter masks corresponding to g' and g'', respectively. A Canny filtering then amounts to performing three separate convolutions with such masks. Clearly, this is equivalent to performing one convolution with a mask obtained by multiplying those three masks. For instance, the mask G defined as

$$G \quad = \quad G_1(x) \cdot G_0(y) \cdot G_0(z).$$

performs a Canny filtering in the x-direction. Figure 7.28 illustrates this point.

In a similar fashion, higher-order partial derivatives can be computed using filter masks obtained from G_0, G_1, G_2 as needed. The masks for computing first- and second-order partial derivatives are listed below:

$$\begin{aligned}
f_x &= I * (G_1(x) \cdot G_0(y) \cdot G_0(z)), \\
f_{xx} &= I * (G_2(x) \cdot G_0(y) \cdot G_0(z)), \\
f_{xy} &= I * (G_1(x) \cdot G_1(y) \cdot G_0(z)),
\end{aligned}$$

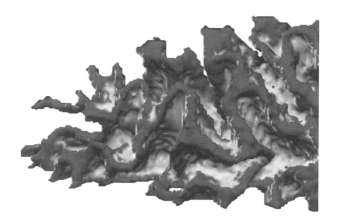

Figure 7.29: Convex (dark) and concave (light) regions

$$
\begin{aligned}
f_y &= I * (G_0(x) \cdot G_1(y) \cdot G_0(z)), \\
f_{yy} &= I * (G_0(x) \cdot G_2(y) \cdot G_0(z)), \\
f_{yz} &= I * (G_0(x) \cdot G_1(y) \cdot G_1(z)), \\
f_z &= I * (G_0(x) \cdot G_0(y) \cdot G_1(z)), \\
f_{zz} &= I * (G_0(x) \cdot G_0(y) \cdot G_2(z)), \\
f_{xz} &= I * (G_1(x) \cdot G_0(y) \cdot G_1(z)).
\end{aligned}
$$

The width of the filter masks depends on the choice of σ. A reasonable choice is for instance $\sigma = 1$ with a mask size of $7 \times 7 \times 7$. Clearly, functions other than the Gaussian and its derivatives may be used to construct the filter masks. Monga et al. [102] suggest using Deriche's filter function as defined in section 7.2.2. They also advise normalizing the filters so that:

$$
\sum_{-r}^{r} G_0(v) = 1,
$$

$$
\sum_{-r}^{r} G_1(v) = 0, \quad \sum_{r} v G_1(v) = 1,
$$

$$
\sum_{-r}^{r} G_2(v) = 0, \quad \sum_{r} \frac{v^2}{2} G_2(v) = 1.
$$

Using the methodology presented so far, we are finally ready to compute curvature properties of a surface. Figure 7.29 for instance shows a classification of a surface according to its curvature type. Only mean curvature was used here. Areas where the mean curvature is negative are shown in dark, positive mean curvature are indicated by a lighter shade of grey. This classification roughly distinguishes convex regions from concave. However, as Gaussian curvature was ignored here, hyperbolic regions are grouped into one of the two classes.

Chapter 8

Region segmentation

The goal of segmentation is to assign a class label to each voxel in an image so that voxels that are similar in some predefined sense are grouped into the same class. Most of the time, the similarity criterion is based on grey values so that voxels having similar grey values receive the same class label. In addition, other criteria such as spatial proximity may be used. A large amount of literature has been published on this topic over recent decades so that an exhaustive account is next to impossible. We will restrict our presentation to some of the most frequently used algorithms with special emphasis on the ones that have been applied to volumetric images. For further reading, see for instance [1], [4].

8.1 Clustering methods

Clustering algorithms group voxels of similar grey value intensity into coherent clusters. In this section, we will present some basic clustering techniques which are quite useful in a number of circumstances. More advanced techniques will be discussed in section 8.2.

8.1.1 Simple thresholding

The easiest method of grouping voxels into classes is simply to threshold their grey values so that all voxels whose grey values are in a given range fall into the same class. Most often, this method is used to binarize an image so that the image foreground is separated from its background.

a) original image   b) threshold set to 80   c) threshold set to 130

Figure 8.1: Thresholding

While this approach is quite effective in many cases, a number of problems may arise. The most notable problem is of course that the choice of the threshold is difficult, and may lead to strange results. Figure 8.1 shows an example of two thresholds applied to an image. Note that different choices of the threshold produce entirely different results.

A great help in choosing an appropriate threshold is the *image histogram*. The histogram records the relative frequencies of each grey value. Figure 8.2 shows the histogram of the image in figure 8.1. Local maxima of the histogram often correspond to objects in the image scene so that thresholds are often best placed at local minima of the histogram to separate the objects.

8.1.2   Unsupervised clustering

The thresholding method introduced in section 8.1.1 is not fully automatic as the choice of the threshold often requires manual intervention. Therefore, so-called *unsupervised clustering* methods have been devised which perform the threshold selection automatically. We will present one of the most well known algorithms – called *ISODATA* [103] – as an example.

Let $x = (x_0, ..., x_n) \in \mathbb{R}^n$ be a *feature vector*. In our context, $x \in \mathbb{R}$ or $x \in [0, ..., 255]$ is a one-dimensional feature vector representing the grey value at some voxel. If a colour image is given with a red, green and blue component, then $x \in \mathbb{R}^3$ may represent the values of the red, green and blue component values of a voxel. The *feature space* is the set of all feature vectors present in an image. Its dimension depends on the

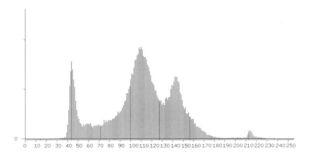

Figure 8.2: A histogram

number of features used. In our context, we have only one measurement at each voxel so that the feature space is one-dimensional and can be visualized by the image histogram. Let

$$S = \{x_l \in \mathbb{R}^n \mid l = 1, .., k\}$$

denote the feature space containing k number of feature vectors. We now want to group these feature vectors into m clusters where $2 \leq m < k$ so that feature vectors belonging to the same cluster exhibit similar feature values. A cluster centre represents the mean value of all feature vectors within that cluster. The ISODATA clustering procedure searches for suitable cluster centres such that the distances between the cluster centres and the members of the clusters are minimized.

ISODATA is an iterative procedure in which at each iteration the cluster centres are updated until convergence is achieved. The number of clusters to be detected is fixed throughout the procedure and must be initially supplied by the user.

Let $\mu_j(i), 1 \leq j \leq m$ denote the jth cluster centre obtained at iteration i. The initial cluster centres $\mu_j(0)$ may be arbitrarily distributed throughout the feature space.

At the ith iteration, we inspect each feature vector x_l in turn and determine the cluster centre closest to it, say $\mu_{j_0}(i)$. We then attribute label j_0 to x_l and recompute the centre of cluster j_0 to account for its new member. This procedure is repeated until the cluster centres remain stable.

Figure 8.3 shows the result of an ISODATA clustering applied to the image of figure 8.1. Four clusters were sought, and their centre were found to be $\mu_1 = 54.39$, $\mu_2 = 106.97$, $\mu_3 = 143.62$, $\mu_4 = 204.40$

Figure 8.3: Result of isodata clustering

which agrees quite well with the local maxima in the image histogram. A proof of the convergence of the ISODATA algorithm is given in [104]. An application to volumetric images is reported in [105].

If the cluster centres cannot be found reliably by an automatic procedure, we should revert to semi-automatic methods or *supervised classification*. The basic idea is to provide training samples for each class so that statistical properties such as mean or covariance can be estimated. Using decision theoretic methods these statistical characteristics can be used to classify the remaining feature vectors which were not in any of the training samples. For more information see for instance [106].

8.2   Contextual segmentation

The procedures presented so far do not use adjacency relations between voxels to determine class labels. However, spatial proximity is quite often an important clue and its use may be helpful. A class of segmentation procedures – called *contextual classification* – specifically addresses this point. The goal of these methods is not primarily to partition the feature space but to partition the image into homogeneous and coherent regions where the homogeneity criterion may vary depending on the task in hand.

8.2.1   Region growing

The simplest method is called *region growing*. It starts out with a set of seed voxels, one for each region. The neighbourhood of each seed is inspected and voxels similar enough to the seed voxel are added to the region represented by its seed. This process is repeated recursively until no further voxels can be added to any region and the accumulation stops. Note that some voxels may remain unlabelled which is not always a problem if for instance only foreground voxels are of interest.

The biggest problem in region growing is the definition of the homogeneity criterion. If it is too restrictive then many voxels will be missed, and if it is too permissive then the region growing may spill over region boundaries and sometimes even flood the entire image. Joliot et al. [107] address this problem in the context of magnetic resonance images.

8.2.2   Hysteresis thresholding

A variation of region growing is *hysteresis thresholding*. We have already discussed it in section 7.4 as a method of edge linking. Clearly, it can also be used in the present context. Remember that hysteresis thresholding requires an upper and a lower threshold for each connected component. In edge linking we used the same upper and lower bounds for all edge components. In the context of region segmentation, we must select different pairs of thresholds for each region. Again, the selection of suitable thresholds is the most difficult part. However, the use of both a lower and an upper threshold makes this choice a little less dramatic, as the two thresholds effectively open a whole range of grey values.

8.2.3   Split-and-merge segmentation

Split-and-merge segmentation works by recursively subdividing the image into smaller subimages until all subimages are homogeneous with respect to some predefined homogeneity criterion. This process is the "splitting" part of the procedure. While it enforces homogeneity within the regions it produces many similar regions which remain separate. To remedy this problem, a merging step is applied which merges adjacent regions into coherent chunks that are similar with respect to the homogeneity criterion.

Clearly, the octree encoding procedure as discussed in section 2.3.3 is ideally suited to the splitting step, which is why octree encodings are often used for this task. Strasters et al. [108], for instance describe such a split-and-merge segmentation based on an octree encoding.

8.2.4   Edge based segmentation

A quite popular segmentation method is based on edge detection using methods we discussed in chapter 7. Bormans et al. [109] and also Ylä-Jääski et al. [110] perform a volumetric segmentation using the Marr-Hildreth edge detector. Remember that the Marr-Hildreth operator works by detecting zero-crossings of the second derivatives. Therefore, it always returns closed boundaries around regions.

This makes it particularly attractive for region segmentation, as edge operators that are based on first derivatives usually do not yield closed boundaries. However, second-order derivatives are more susceptible to noise, so that there are pros and cons for both sides.

Liou at al. [111] use first-order derivatives to obtain hypothetical region boundaries. They determine minimal thresholds on the edge strengths required to partition the volumetric image into homogeneous regions which they call α-solids. The α-solids give an initial α-partitioning of the image space. A subsequent volume filtering step removes remaining errors incurred during the first step.

8.2.5   Other algorithms

The above list of segmentation algorithms is by no means complete. In fact, segmentation is one of the most difficult problems in image analysis, and many different attempts at solving this problem have been made. Spatial proximity, for instance, has been modelled using Markov random fields [112], [113].

Another type of algorithm specifically addresses the problem of grey level variations across the image. This problems arises when owing to some external influence during the image acquisition process some portions of the image appear lighter or darker than others, so that the same object shows up differently at different image locations. The method described by Wells et at. [114] is an example of such an algorithm.

In recent years, another class of algorithm aimed at fitting parametric models to image data has gained a lot of interest. We will discuss this approach in more detail in chapter 10 where it will be presented in the context of surface reconstruction.

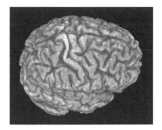

Figure 8.4: A volume rendering of a human brain data set

8.3   An application: extracting the brain from an MR data set

To demonstrate applications of a number of the algorithms we have encountered so far, let us look at a "real-life" example of a 3D image analysis task. Suppose we have acquired magnetic resonance data of some healthy subject, and we now want to visualize the brain surface. The first obstacle we must overcome is to remove the skull and other tissue surrounding the brain from our data set because they block the view towards the brain. The problem of extracting the brain from an MR data set is sometimes called "brain-peeling" [115], [116]. Brain peeling is performed by successively applying several of the image analysis algorithms we have discussed so far.

Figure 8.4 shows the volume rendering we want to obtain[1]. The

---

[1]For more on rendering techniques see appendix A.

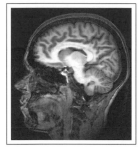   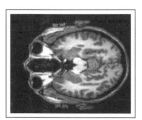   

a) input slice (vertical)   b) input slice (horizontal)   c) segmentation

Figure 8.5: Brain peeling: the first steps

input image in this particular case consist of 256 slices each having 192 rows and 256 columns. Figures 8.5a,b illustrate the problem: the original image contains a lot of tissue that we do not want to see.

We begin by applying an unsupervised clustering such as ISODATA to obtain a coarse outline of the brain. Unfortunately, the brain has approximately the same grey value as some other non-brain tissues which therefore remain attached to the brain after segmentation (see figure 8.5c).

To separate brain from non-brain tissue, we erode the image using either a morphological erosion filter with a sphere-shaped structuring element of some small size, or – alternatively – threshold the distance transform as discussed in section 4.5. Figure 8.6a shows the result.

There are still some portions of non-brain tissue around but they are no longer connected to the brain. Thus, we perform a connected component labelling using one of our algorithms of section 2.2 and select the largest of them hoping that it will correspond to the brain.

During the erosion operation we have not only separated brain from non-brain tissue but unfortunately we have removed some brain tissue as well. So the final step in our processing chain consists in restoring those portions by reverting the erosion using a morphological dilation. Since non-brain parts have already been removed at this stage, there is no danger of reconnecting the brain to non-brain parts at this point. The final result is shown in figure 8.6c.

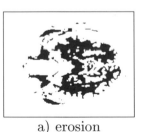  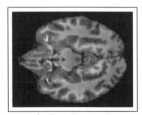

a) erosion   b) the largest component   c) final result

Figure 8.6: Brain peeling: the final steps

Part III

Modelling and Registration of Objects

In this third part of the book we will talk about modelling and registration of objects. Both topics are relevant to object recognition. Object modelling aims at finding higher-level representations of objects so that they can be matched against entries in an object database. Registration refers to the problem of geometrically aligning either volumetric images or object models to facilitate comparisons.

In the first two chapters of this part we will mainly discuss boundary representations of objects. Suppose some object has been extracted from an image by one of the segmentation algorithms introduced in the previous chapter so that we have a binary image in which the foreground has been successfully separated from the background. We are now seeking alternative representations for such an image. In section 2.3 we already introduced the octree and track representation schemes. But these representations are not adequate in many situations. An alternative to these elementary methods are so-called *boundary representations* or *b-reps* for short. As the name implies, an object encoded by a boundary representation is only represented by its enclosing surface.

B-reps are often not exact in the sense that the enclosing boundary used for representation fits the object somewhat loosely. This is quite often a desired effect, especially where smooth boundaries are preferable. This may for instance be the case when differential properties – such as curvature – must be computed, or when the object is to be prepared for graphics rendering.

Another reason why approximate boundaries may be preferable is that the segmentation may be faulty owing to noise in the image data, or even worse, the segmentation may be incomplete so that only a certain fraction of the border points are known. In this case, we may want to reconstruct the surface by approximating it using some smooth function which recovers the "true" surface that is hidden somewhere among the noise.

In addition, special b-reps exist which represent the object at a much higher level of abstraction and are therefore useful for object recognition purposes. In this chapter, we will discuss various surface representation schemes and discuss how they can be made to fit the image data.

Chapter 9

Surface tiling

A frequently used b-rep scheme represents objects by a *polygonal mesh* consisting of vertices, edges and faces. Figure 9.1 shows an example. The faces of such meshes are planar patches bounded by closed polygons such that adjacent faces share exactly one polygonal edge and its two vertices. The faces of polygonal meshes have a fixed number of vertices – three or four are typical choices.

The process of producing such a mesh from a given volumetric data set depicting one or several objects is called *surface tiling*, because the objects will be covered with a layer of "tiles". A large number of surface tiling methods have been reported in the literature of which we will present a few examples.

9.1 Boundary tracking

Let us begin with a well known algorithm which produces a list of square faces which correspond to the voxel faces visible from the "outside". It performs what is called a *boundary tracking* of the object. Boundary tracking differs from the border detection algorithm we presented in section 2.1.3 in several respects. Firstly, boundary tracking delivers the visible *faces* of voxels, not the voxels themselves. Secondly, boundary tracking traverses each connected component separately, in contrast to border detection which scans the entire image irrespective of connectivities.

One of the first boundary tracking algorithms goes back to Artzy et al. [117]. Later revisions and improvements are reported in [118]

Figure 9.1: A polyhedral mesh

and [119]. The basic idea is to track the boundary in a breadth first traversal, where each time a visible face is found it is written into an output list.

We begin by manually identifying a "seed" node which is some arbitrary visible face of a voxel. We then inspect its neighbourhood to identify any other visible faces adjacent to the first face. Any visible face that is found is placed into the output list and into a queue Q of nodes yet to be processed. Nodes in Q are successively dequeued and processed by placing visible faces adjacent to them into Q. Each time a node is processed it is marked as "visited" to prevent it from being processed twice. The algorithm terminates when the queue Q becomes empty. Below, a pseudocode version is given.

```
Queue Q; /* queue of nodes to be processed */
List M; /* list of marked nodes */
Node n0: /* seed node */

put n0 into Q and M;
while (Q not empty) {
   dequeue a node n from Q;
   output n;
   for each neighbour m of n {
      if m not in M then {
         put m in M and Q
      }
   }
}
```

The algorithm is often used for visualizing voxel images. However,

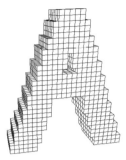

Figure 9.2: A tiling produced by boundary tracking

the surfaces of objects appear quite ragged owing to the raggedness of the voxel grid. Figure 9.2 shows an object displayed in this way.

To obtain surfaces that appear more natural triangular meshes are more suitable. In the following, algorithms for computing triangular meshes will be presented.

9.2 The marching cubes algorithm

The most well known algorithm for surface triangulation is perhaps the *marching cubes algorithm* devised by Lorensen and Cline [120]. The basic idea is the following. Consider a cube whose vertices are defined by eight voxels which are mutually 6-adjacent and arranged as follows [1]:

The algorithm proceeds by inspecting each such cube within the image lattice while trying to determine if and where the object surface intersects the cube. For instance, the above configuration suggests that the object surface is located as shown below:

---

[1]Remember that foreground voxels are displayed in black, and background voxels are white.

Note that any such polygonal patch can be easily decomposed into several triangles so that a surface triangulation can be obtained from such patches. The marching cubes algorithm inspects each cube and attributes a surface patch to it. Theoretically, there are $256 = 2^8$ different configurations of black and white voxels conceivable within a cube. Exploiting the symmetry of the cube, only 22 different configurations remain. Of these 22 cases, another 8 can be omitted because they are just the exact inverses of some of other configuration, so that 14 principal configurations remain. Figure 9.3 shows the complete assembly of these configurations.

These cases can be listed in a look-up table, so that each time a cube is inspected, we only need to search the look-up table to determine its surface patch. The marching cubes algorithm proceeds as follows: we scan the entire image starting with the top left corner of the first slice working our way towards the second-last slice. Each time we encounter a foreground voxel, we inspect the eight-voxel cube to which the current voxel belongs, look up its configuration in our table and produce the corresponding triangulation of this cube.

Unfortunately though, the exact location of the surface is not always clear from the configuration of black voxels within the cube as the following example shows:

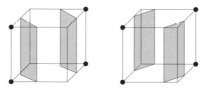

Both surface configurations are conceivable and the ambiguity cannot be easily resolved. As a result, the marching cubes algorithm is not guaranteed to produce a closed surface as the following example shows:

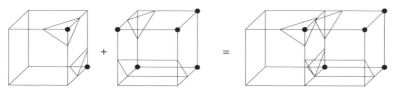

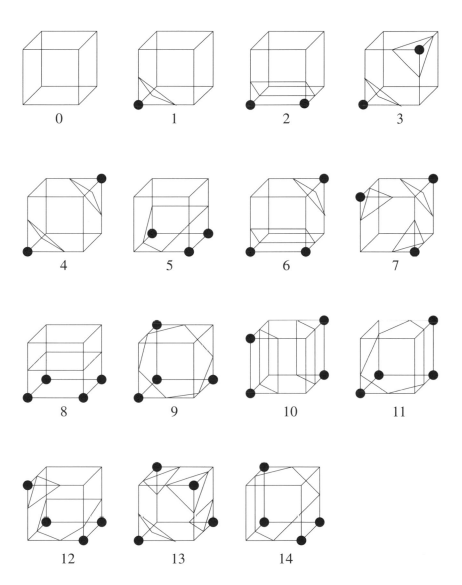

Figure 9.3: The marching cubes configurations

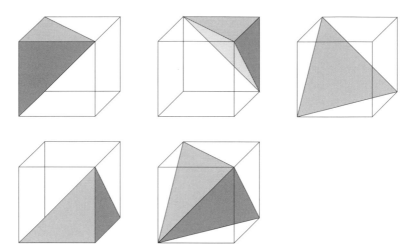

Figure 9.4: Cell decomposition by five tetrahedra

9.3   The wrapper algorithm

In the following, we will present another surface tiling algorithm – called the *wrapper algorithm* [121] – which elegantly circumvents the problems of the marching cubes algorithm so that a closed and complete triangulation of the surface is guaranteed. Its disadvantage is that it usually produces up to three times more triangles and therefore often requires a postprocessing step for mesh simplification which reduces the number of triangles to an acceptable level.

As before, the surface to be tiled is given as an iso-value such that voxels whose grey values fall below the threshold are considered to be exterior, and the others are considered to be interior. The algorithm begins by partitioning the voxel lattice into cubes each consisting of eight 6-adjacent voxels, exactly like the cubes we have already encountered in the previous section. Each cube is then subpartitioned into five tetrahedra as shown in figure 9.4 – four of which have edges of equal length, the fifth has faces of equal size.

There are two alternative ways in which tetrahedral decomposition of a cube can be organized (see figure 9.5), which are called "even" and "odd" for lack of a better word. The voxel lattice is partitioned into an alternating pattern of even and odd cubes much like a checkerboard. This ensures that the tetrahedra in adjacent cells match so that

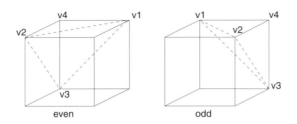

Figure 9.5: Two alternative cell decompositions

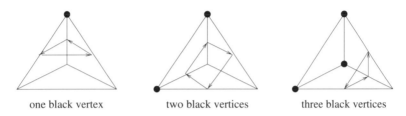

Figure 9.6: Three cases of surface intersections

ultimately a consistent surface results.

The next step consists in determining if and where the surface intersects a tetrahedron. Note that exactly four voxels belong to one tetrahedron. If all four voxels are interior or if no voxel is interior then the surface does not intersect this tetrahedron, and we may ignore it. Let us look at the remaining three cases: there may be either one, two or three interior voxels left. We must now estimate the exact location where the surface intersects the edges of the polyhedron.

The simplest approach is to use a linear interpolation between each pair of vertices to approximate the surface intersection point at the edge connecting the pair of vertices. Better results are obtained by using bilinear interpolation involving all four vertices. Let (a, b, c, d) denote the intensity values at the four vertices. The bilinear interpolation is identical to the simple linear interpolation for the 6-adjacent vertices. For the diagonal edges however, the following interpolation formula results:

$$I(u) \ = \ (a \ + \ d \ - \ c)^2 u^2 \ + \ (-2a \ + \ b \ + \ c)u \ + \ a$$

where the parameter u varies from 0 to 1 along the diagonal. The intersection point is obtained by computing a value u_0 for which $I(u_0) = 0$.

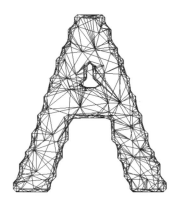

Figure 9.7: A triangulation produced by the wrapper

The intersection points determine the vertices of the surface tiles as shown in figure 9.6. Note that the surface tiles are oriented as indicated by the arrows. The orientation helps to differentiate between the interior and the exterior side of each surface tile. By convention, when viewed from the outside, the orientation is counterclockwise. To ensure a consistent object topology, this convention must be enforced throughout the entire surface mesh.

9.4   Surfaces from planar contours

The surface tiling methods we have discussed so far presuppose that a voxel data structure is given which depicts one or several solid objects. Sometimes however, we must derive a surface tiling when we do not have access to such a straightforward object representation. This is the case when the object is given only as a set of planar contours which are obtained by intersecting the object's surface with a set of parallel planes. Each contour is represented as a closed polygon whose vertices need not be equally spaced.

Deriving a surface tiling from planar contours is much more difficult than deriving it from raster images. Figure 9.8 illustrates the difficulties inherent in this problem. The first problem we encounter – called the *correspondence problem* – is to identify corresponding contours in adjacent slices. It may be difficult if there is more than one contour in both slices. If the inter-slice distance is small the contours will not be

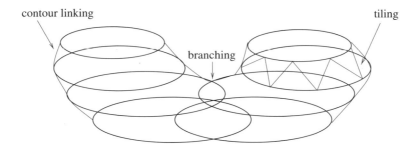

Figure 9.8: Surface tiling from planar contours

too different, and a match can be easily found. If however the slices are far apart and the object is a complicated knot then it may be next to impossible to follow individual strands of the knot from one slice to the next.

Several approaches to the automatic solution of the correspondence problem are conceivable [122]. For instance, we may try to simplify the problem by first fitting a two-dimensional ellipse to each contour and then linking the ellipses into elliptical cylinders in a process called "cylinder growing". The correspondence problem becomes a lot more tractable this way as cylinders can be represented by a lot fewer parameters than polygons. However, there is no guarantee that this approach will always produce a correct result.

The second problem we must solve – provided the correspondence problem has been successfully dealt with – is the *tiling problem*, which consists in triangulating the area spanned between two corresponding contours in adjacent slices. The basic idea is to generate a mesh of triangles that is optimal with respect to some predefined criterion. For instance, we may want to produce a mesh whose surface area is minimal.

The third problem – called the *branching problem* – arises when a contour splits up into two or more contours from one slice to the next. A possible solution to this problem comes from the area of computational geometry. Boissonnat [123] has suggested using Delaunay triangulation in this context which produces a triangular mesh from a given set of input vertices. We will not go into further detail at this point. For more detail on Delaunay triangulation see for instance [124].

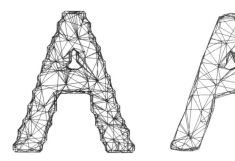

Figure 9.9: A surface mesh and its simplification

9.5   Mesh simplification

Surface meshes often contain a very large number of polygons – sometimes as many as tens of thousands – so that they can be quite awkward to handle. In such cases a process called *mesh simplification* is required. In mesh simplification we try to decimate the mesh by deleting as many polygons as possible without altering the topology of the original mesh and without changing its geometrical shape too much. The degree to which the shape is allowed to vary is usually an input parameter into the algorithm. Figure 9.9 shows a mesh produced by the wrapper algorithm and its simplification produced by the algorithm described in [121].

The basic idea underlying most mesh simplification schemes is the following: we inspect each vertex or edge to determine its geometrical and topological properties. If it fulfils a given set of criteria, it is deleted from the mesh. Finally, the resulting hole is patched by a new triangulation containing fewer triangles. One pass through the entire net will usually decimate the mesh to some extent. To achieve higher compression rates, this process is iterated until no further deletions are possible.

The various mesh simplification schemes differ in whether vertices, edges or even entire faces are deleted. They also differ in their deletion criteria, and in their methods of hole patching. Schroeder et al. [125] for instance, have devised an algorithm which deletes vertices rather than edges. The deletion criteria they use include a "distance-to-plane" criterion, which measures the distance of the vertex from an hypothetical average plane through the triangle. If this distance is small enough, the

Figure 9.10: Deletion of an edge in mesh simplification

vertex may be deleted.

The method proposed by Gueziec at al. [121] deletes edges instead of vertices. In deleting an edge from the mesh two vertices are replaced by one new vertex as shown in figure 9.10. Various deletion criteria are used in the process.

An entirely different approach is used by Hoppe at al. [126]. Their method not only deletes points from the mesh but it also allows points to change their locations. They formulate mesh simplification as an optimization problem in which goodness of fit to the original data competes with data compression.

Chapter 10

Surface reconstruction

So far we have discussed methods for deriving surfaces of objects which were already segmented by some previous segmentation routine, or which could easily be described by an iso-value or threshold. Many times however, life is not so easy. In analysing images we often encounter the problem that object boundaries are vague and not clearly definable by thresholds. In such situations, we need to perform an operation called *surface reconstruction*. In surface reconstruction, a surface is recovered from scattered and unordered data points. Missing points must be inserted using some interpolation scheme.

In order to be able to make an informed guess about suitable locations for missing data points on the surface, we must use additional information from other sources. The most frequently used approach is to make assumptions about the smoothness and connectedness of the surface we want to recover. For instance, we may want to assume that the surface is differentiable everywhere, or even more stringently that it obeys some particular parametric form. We may want to impose the constraint that the surface must be a planar patch or that it must be quadratic polynomial in which case it could be locally described as:

$$S(u,v) \; = \; (u, v, au^2 + 2buv + cv^2).$$

Parametric models not only have the advantage of allowing surface reconstruction, but in addition they present a much more condensed representation than polygonal meshes. For instance, if we assume that the entire surface is given globally by a quadratic polynomial, then we would need no more than the three parameters a, b, c to represent it

as opposed to the many triangles that would be required for a polygonal mesh. Clearly, this is a major advantage in many respects. Not
only does it require less storage space, but it also makes it possible to
identify and classify surfaces by their parametric form so that they can
be matched against entries in a database. Thus, parametric representations are an important step not only towards surface reconstruction
but in some cases also towards object recognition.

Let us begin by formalizing what we mean by "parametric models".
Generally speaking, parametric models describe an object in terms of
a few parameters such as the three parameters of a quadratic patch
mentioned above. They can be given in any one of the following mathematical formulations.

Firstly, a parametric model

$$f : U \subset \mathbb{R}^n \to \mathbb{R}$$

may be given in *explicit form* by its graph:

$$graph(f) \; = \; \{(u_1, ..., u_n, f(u_1, ..., u_n)) \mid (u_1, ., ,, u_n) \in U\}.$$

If the model defines a surface, then $n = 2$. A curve is defined by a
function whose domain has dimension one, and a volume has dimension
three.

Alternatively, a model g may be given in *implicit form* as the set of
values fulfilling a defining equation:

$$g : \; \mathbb{R}^{n+1} \to \mathbb{R}$$

$$\{(x_1, ..., x_{n+1}) \in \mathbb{R}^{n+1} \mid g(x_1, ..., x_{n+1}) = 0\}.$$

Note that the implicit form requires a function whose domain has a
higher dimensionality than the explicit form. Thus, a surface is defined
by a function whose domain has dimension three, and so forth.

Unfortunately, the two forms are not always interchangeable. In
fact, the explicit form can always be transformed into the implicit form,
but not vice versa. Thus, the implicit form is more general.

For closed surfaces the implicit form has the advantage of being able
to define the volume enclosed by a surface in a quite natural way. We
only have to replace "=" by "≤" to obtain the enclosed volume:

$$\{(x_1, ..., x_{n+1}) \in \mathbb{R}^{n+1} \mid g(x_1, ..., x_{n+1}) \leq 0\}.$$

In addition to the implicit and the explicit form, there exists a third form of representation called the *parametric form*. A parametric form representing a surface is given by a function

$$f : U \subset \mathbb{R}^2 \to \mathbb{R}^3$$

so that $f(u, v)$ consists of three components:

$$f(u, v) = (f_0(u, v), f_1(u, v), f_2(u, v)).$$

In the following, we will discuss a few models which are common in 3D image analysis and present their use for surface representation and recovery. We will concentrate on the description of surfaces and volumes and ignore space curves.

10.1 Parametric forms

Parametric forms are often given in the following way:

$$f(u, v) = \sum_{i=1}^{n} \bar{V}_i \, g_i(u, v) \in \mathbb{R}^3, \; u, v \in [0, 1]. \qquad (10.1)$$

where $g_i(u, v)$ are some basis functions, and $\bar{V}_i = (v_{i0}, v_{i1}, v_{i2}) \in \mathbb{R}^3$ are control points that determine the shape locally. The various models differ in the choice of their basis functions.

10.1.1 Rational Gaussian surfaces

A *Rational Gaussian surface (RaG)* [127] is a special instance of the general form given in equation 10.1. It is defined as:

$$f(u, v) \stackrel{\text{def}}{=} \sum_{i=1}^{n} \bar{V}_i \, g_i(u, v), \; u, v \in [0, 1].$$

where the basis functions are Gaussians given by:

$$g_i(u, v) \stackrel{\text{def}}{=} \frac{W_i \, G_i(u, v)}{\sum_{j=1}^{n} W_j \, G_j(u, v)}$$

and

$$G_i(u, v) \stackrel{\text{def}}{=} \exp(-[(u - u_i)^2 + (v - v_i)^2]/(2\sigma_i^2)).$$

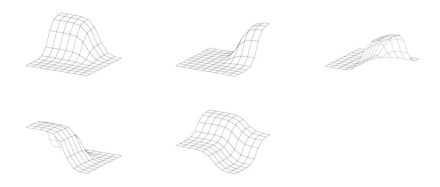

Figure 10.1: RaG surfaces

The points $\bar{V}_i = (v_{i0}, v_{i1}, v_{i2}) \in \mathbb{R}^3, i = 1, ..., n$ are control points, which play a decisive role in determining the shape of the surface. In fact, the surface approximates these controls points as closely as possible. The smoothness in the vicinity of each control point V_i is determined by the parameter σ_i so that the smoothness may vary across the surface. In some parts it may be required that we fit the control points closely, which usually implies a small value of σ_i, in others a coarse fit may be desired, implying a high degree of smoothness.

For each control point $\bar{V}_i, i = 1, ..., n$ a node point (u_i, v_i) and a weight W_i must be given. The weights determine the relative strength of each control point within the surface. A high weight at one control point forces the surface towards this point. Figure 10.1 shows a few RaG surfaces which may serve as basis functions.

Rational Gaussian surfaces can be used for surface reconstruction. Remember that in surface reconstruction, we try to fit a surface to a set of unordered scattered data points. Using RaG surfaces, the data points may be represented by the control points of the RaG surface.

Note that surface representations in parametric form require that the node points are ordered. Generally they should be spaced evenly across the range $[0, 1] \times [0, 1]$. Thus, the data points must be ordered as well. There is no simple general solution to the problem of ordering and determining spatial relationships between the data points.

Goshtasby [127] suggest the following approach to be used for points scattered around an object contour given in consecutive slices of a 3D

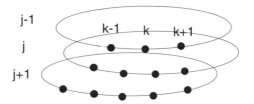

Figure 10.2: Placing nodes onto contours in consecutive slices

image. Let m denote the number of slices in the image, indexed by $j = 0, ..., m - 1$, and let n_j denote the number of data points along the jth contour, indexed by $k = 0, ..., (n_j - 1)$ as illustrated in figure 10.2. Then the control points are given as:

$$u_i = \frac{k}{n_j - 1},$$

$$v_i = \frac{j}{m - 1}.$$

Clearly, this approach only works if correspondences between contours in consecutive slices are known, which is the case if for instance only one cylindrical object is given. The data points may be scattered around the contour. We have already encountered a similar problem in section 9.4 where correspondences between adjacent contours had to be found.

10.1.2 Second-order polynomials

A special case that we have encountered before is that of the *second-order polynomial functions*:

$$f(u, v) = (u, v, au^2 + 2buv + cv^2).$$

Sander et al. [128] have used them to obtain local surface patches to be used for curvature computations (see also section 7.5). Note that quite often we cannot represent an entire surface by just one such function. Instead we need to apply a different quadratic patch at each point on the surface, and then glue all local patches together to form a coherent fabric.

10.1.3   Other parametric forms

As it would be impossible to discuss all relevant parametric forms in depth, we will conclude this section by listing a few well known models. For an excellent review see for instance Besl [129].

A parametric model closely related to RaG surfaces is the *B-spline surfaces*. They are mostly used to obtain local surface patches. They play a major role in computer graphics applications as well as in surface reconstruction tasks. Using Bernstein polynomials as basis functions in equation 10.1 we obtain *Bezier patches* which are also mostly used in computer graphics and CAD applications [130, p.521 ff.]. Other frequently used models are the so-called non-uniform rational B-spline surfaces or *NURBS* for short. Another well-known parametric model is the *thin-plate-spline* model as introduced by Bookstein [131].

10.2   Implicit forms

Implicit models are given as solutions to a defining equation. Depending on the task in hand this may be more convenient than the parametric representation discussed so far. For instance, using an implicit representation, it is trivial to determine whether or not a point is on the surface: all we have to do is to insert the point coordinates into the implicit equation and test for zero. Likewise, it is trivial to test whether the point is an interior point of the object enclosed by an implicitly defined surface.

Using a parametric form, such a test is not nearly as easy. On the other hand, parametric forms are usually easier to plot. In the following, we will discuss some implicit models which have been used for image analysis.

10.2.1   Quadrics

Quadric surfaces are defined implicitly as the set of solutions to a quadratic polynomial equation of the following form [130, p.528]:

$$
\begin{aligned}
f(x,y,z) \;=\; & a_0 x^2 + a_1 y^2 + a_2 z^2 + 2a_3 xy + 2a_4 yz + 2a_5 xz \\
& + 2a_6 x + 2a_7 y + 2a_8 z + a_9 \;=\; 0.
\end{aligned}
$$

$$(10.2)$$

Figure 10.3: A quadric

Quadrics can be used to represent a large number of well known objects. For instance, a cone may be represented by the quadric:

$$\frac{x^2}{a^2} + \frac{y^2}{b^2} - \frac{z^2}{c^2} = 0,$$

and an ellipsoid is given by:

$$\frac{x^2}{a^2} + \frac{y^2}{b^2} + \frac{z^2}{c^2} = 1.$$

Quadrics are quite popular in a variety of domains, especially in Computer Aided Design and computer graphics because of their many useful properties.

In our context though, we are interested in quadrics as a means of surface reconstruction, and indeed quadrics have been used for this purpose as well [132]. In the following, we will briefly present an approach introduced by Cernusch-Frias [133]. Let

$$S = \{(x_i, y_i, z_i) \mid i = 1, ..., n\}$$

be a set of data points believed to be scattered around the quadric surface we want to recover. If all of these points were exactly located on the quadric, then each of them should obey equation 10.2 so that taken collectively, we should have:

$$\sum_{i=1}^{n} f(x_i, y_i, z_i) = 0,$$

where f is defined as in 10.2. In order to recover a quadric from the set S, we need to estimate the set of parameters $\bar{a} = (a_0, ..., a_9)$ that define its shape. This task can be cast into an optimization problem where

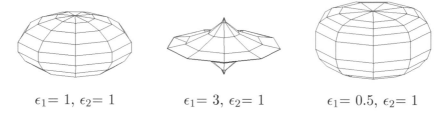

$$\epsilon_1 = 1,\ \epsilon_2 = 1 \qquad\qquad \epsilon_1 = 3,\ \epsilon_2 = 1 \qquad\qquad \epsilon_1 = 0.5,\ \epsilon_2 = 1$$

Figure 10.4: Superquadrics

we need to find the set of values for all parameters that minimizes the term:

$$\arg\min_{\bar{a}} = \sum_{i=1}^{n} [f(x_i, y_i, z_i; \bar{a})]^2.$$

Unfortunately, minimizing this function will not always guarantee a useful result as the trivial solution $\bar{a} = 0$ may be obtained. To avoid problems like this, the set of allowable solutions must be constrained. Cernusch-Frias [133] suggest imposing the following constraint:

$$a_0^2 + a_1^2 + a_2^2 + 2(a_3 + a_4 + a_5) = 2,$$

which excludes the trivial solution and also ensures certain other useful properties of the resulting quadric. Thus, the problem of fitting a quadric to a set of sparse data points is reduced to a constrained minimization problem, which may be solved using some standard approach.

10.2.2 Superquadrics

Superquadrics are extensions of the quadric models introduced in the previous section. They were made popular for surface reconstruction by Pentland [134], and later by Bajcsy [135], [136], and Terzopoulos [137].

Superquadrics are mostly described in their implicit form :

$$f(x,y,z) = \left(\left(\frac{x}{a}\right)^{2/\epsilon_1} + \left(\frac{y}{b}\right)^{2/\epsilon_2} \right)^{\epsilon_2/\epsilon_1} + \left(\frac{z}{c}\right)^{2/\epsilon_1} = 1.$$

However, there also exists a parametric form defined as:

$$g(\eta, \omega) = \begin{bmatrix} a_1 \cos^{\epsilon_1} \eta \ \cos^{\epsilon_2} \omega \\ a_2 \cos^{\epsilon_1} \eta \ \sin^{\epsilon_2} \omega \\ a_3 \sin^{\epsilon_1} \eta \end{bmatrix}$$

where
$$-\frac{\pi}{2} \le \eta \le \frac{\pi}{2}, \text{ and } -\pi \le \omega \le \pi.$$

The two parameters ϵ_1, ϵ_2 control the squareness of the shape. For example, if $\epsilon_1 = \epsilon_2 = 1$ then the resulting superquadric is formed like an ellipsoid. A great variety of shapes can be constructed by using different values for ϵ_1 and ϵ_2. Figure 10.4 shows three examples.

The implicit equation partitions the space into three regions:

if $f(x, y, z) < 1$ then the point (x, y, z) is inside the object, if $f(x, y, z) > 1$ then (x, y, z) is outside, and if $f(x, y, z) = 1$, then the point is on the surface.

Fitting a superquadric to a given set of data points involves several steps: we must first coarsely align the object with the data points by rotating and shifting the model in the general direction of the points, and we must then find good estimates of the models parameters.

Bajcsy and Solina [135], [136] use the following procedure for model fitting. They start out with an initial elliptical superquadric using $\epsilon_1 = \epsilon_2 = 1$. This initial model is shifted so that its centre of gravity coincides with the centre of gravity of the points to be fitted. An initial orientation is determined from the inertia matrix of the data points (see section 3.3).

Translation and rotation are described by an additional six parameters: three translation parameters (t_1, t_2, t_3), and three rotational (ϕ, ρ, ψ) parameters. So altogether there are eleven parameters to be estimated:
$$\bar{a} = (a_1, a_2, a_3, \epsilon_1, \epsilon_2, t_1, t_2, t_3, \phi, \rho, \psi).$$

Thus, the problem of fitting a superquadric consists in finding the minimum of the following term:

$$F(\bar{a}) = \sum_{i=1}^{n} (1 - f(x_i; \bar{a}))^2,$$

which amounts to a non-linear multidimensional optimization problem. Bajcsy and Solina [135], [136] suggest using the Levenberg-Marquardt algorithm [138] for solving this problem.

Even though superquadrics represent a wide range of shapes they are still too coarse in most circumstances so that after fitting a superquadric, refinements are added. Bajcsy and Solina [135], [136] use global deformations such as bending and tapering.

10.2.3   Deformable models

Recently, another powerful approach to object reconstruction was developed which is based on a physical model of deformation. The basic idea is the following: as before, some parametric or free-form surface model is given. The initial model surface is first aligned coarsely with the image data. To obtain a better fit, the points on the surface are drawn towards feature points of the image data acting as forces on the surface. These forces are represented by an *external energy function*. Thus, the model surface is attracted towards the data points. To counterbalance these forces, the model itself has a certain stiffness that prevents it from being pulled completely out of shape. This stiffness is represented by an *internal energy function*. The deformation process consists in minimizing both the internal and external energy functions.

An example of this type of method is the algorithm introduced by Terzopoulos [137]. He used superquadrics as an initial model shape. But in addition to the global deformations discussed in the previous section such as bending and tapering, he also allows local deformations driven by image forces. The deformation parameters are derived at the same time as the model parameters so that the resulting shapes retain some kind of memory of shape.

Other examples of deformable models can be found in [139], [140], [141]. The initial idea goes back to Kass et al. [142]. Since then, the interest in this topic has grown so rapidly that a complete reference list is impossible to compile. See also [143] for an alternative approach using point distribution models.

Chapter 11

Registration

In many applications, several data sets must be evaluated and compared. In order to do so the data sets must be geometrically aligned or superimposed. A great variety of approaches for solving this problem exists. Each technique is characterized by the following four components [144]:

- a feature space,

- a search space,

- a search strategy,

- a similarity metric.

The feature space determines which features are used for registration. In some cases, lines or points are used for matching. In other approaches, entire voxel images are registered. The search space limits the possibility of choices that have to be considered in the process so that the search for solutions becomes feasible. The search strategy refers to the specific methods used for scanning the search space. Finally, the similarity metric tells us when a match is found.

To simplify the presentation, we will begin with a very easy type of feature spaces that are simply sets of points. In the second part, we will address techniques of geometrically transforming entire voxel images (not just sets of points). Those two types of problem are closely linked: imagine that you first extract sets of salient points from two voxel images and compute parameters of a geometric transformation that aligns those two point sets. In a second step, you then use those same parameters to align the entire voxel images. However, there are also other techniques for aligning voxel images, which we will present in due course. Excellent reviews of registration methods are given in [145] and [144].

11.1   Affine linear transformations of point sets

Let us begin by discussing the problem of aligning two sets of points. You may think of these points as having been extracted from voxel images in some previous processing step, either manually or by some automatic procedure. Sometimes the identification of reference points is facilitated by fixing external markers to the object prior to image acquisition, so that these points show up prominently in the image. But markers are often too invasive and cannot be easily placed in appropriate positions. If markers cannot be used, reference points must be identified by some other means. Let us assume that this problem has somehow been solved, and we are now trying to identify a geometric transformation that aligns the two sets.

Figure 11.1 shows two point sets before and after registration. In this particular case registration was achieved by a 90^0 rotation and a translation.

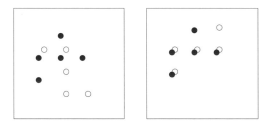

Figure 11.1: Two point sets before and after registration

Suppose the coordinates of two sets of data points U and X are given, where each set has n number of points:

$$U = \{u_i, i = 0, 1, 2, .., n\} \text{ and } X = \{x_i, i = 0, 1, 2, .., n\}.$$

Each pair of points u_i, x_i has m coordinates $u_i = (u_{i1}, u_{i2}, .., u_{im})$, $x_i =$

$(x_{i1}, x_{i2}, .., x_{im})$. For ease of presentation let us assume for the moment that $m = 2$.

Further suppose that we also know correspondences between these points. In particular, we know that point u_i in the first data set corresponds to point x_i in the second data set. Such correspondences may have been established manually or they may have resulted from some automatic procedure.

We now want to align these two point sets so that they overlap as closely as possible. We therefore need to find the parameters of a geometric transformation that produces such an alignment. This is a lot easier if we know the type of transformation underlying the process.

The simplest assumption that we can make in this regard is that the transformation is affine linear. Linear affine transformations encompass scaling, shifting, rotating or reflecting coordinates of points. A characteristic property of these transformations is that the collinearity of points is preserved, i.e. points that were collinear prior to the transformation (lying on the same straight line) will remain collinear after the transformation. In the following, we will discuss methods of estimating the parameters of such transformations.

If our assumption about the linearity of the transformation is correct, then the following relationship holds for each pair of points $u_i, x_i, i = 0, 1, 2, ..., n$:

$$u_i = Bx_i + t \tag{11.1}$$

for some 2×2 matrix B and some translation vector t. Sometimes, it is useful to put the translation vector and the matrix B into a single combined matrix A as follows:

$$A = \begin{bmatrix} t_0 & b_{00} & b_{01} \\ t_1 & b_{10} & b_{11} \end{bmatrix} = \begin{bmatrix} a_{00} & a_{01} & a_{02} \\ a_{10} & a_{11} & a_{12} \end{bmatrix} \tag{11.2}$$

Rewriting equation 11.1 accordingly yields (for $i = 0, 1, 2, ..., n$):

$$u_{i0} = a_{00} + a_{01}x_{i0} + a_{02}x_{i1}$$
$$u_{i1} = a_{10} + a_{11}x_{i0} + a_{12}x_{i1}$$

Rearranging terms, we can express this relationship somewhat differently in matrix notation as follows (for simplicity, we only present the case for three points indexed by $i = 0, 1, 2$):

$$\begin{bmatrix} u_{0j} \\ u_{1j} \\ u_{2j} \end{bmatrix} = \begin{bmatrix} 1 & x_{00} & x_{01} \\ 1 & x_{10} & x_{11} \\ 1 & x_{20} & x_{21} \end{bmatrix} \begin{bmatrix} a_{j0} \\ a_{j1} \\ a_{j2} \end{bmatrix} \quad \text{for } j = 0, 1.$$

Let

$$P = \begin{bmatrix} 1 & x_{00} & x_{01} \\ 1 & x_{10} & x_{11} \\ 1 & x_{20} & x_{21} \end{bmatrix}$$

so that equation 11.1 now reads:

$$u^j = P a^j, \quad j = 0, 1$$

where the index $u_j, j = 0, 1$ denotes the column vector of the jth coordinate of all points in U, i.e.

$$u^j = \begin{bmatrix} u_{0j} \\ u_{1j} \\ u_{2j} \end{bmatrix}.$$

Likewise, $a^j, j = 0, 1$ denotes the row vector of the j-th row of A. Note that we need at least three point pairs to solve this equation.

Generally, we do not know whether a matrix A exists such that the above equations hold for all coordinates of all points. But we can estimate values for the matrix A such that this relationship holds as closely as possible. To achieve this we need to find values for a^j that minimize the term

$$\| u^j - P a^j \|^2, \quad j = 0, 1. \tag{11.3}$$

Problems like these can be solved using so-called *least squares estimation* techniques, of which many different versions are known. Perhaps the most widely used technique is based on a singular value decomposition which gives a direct, non-iterative way of finding the minimum value of the above expression [138, p. 676–680]. We will not go into more detail at this point, but refer the interested reader to the abundant literature that exists on this topic.

11.2   Rigid transformations of point sets

The method described in the previous section is useful when a general affine linear transformation is sought.

Sometimes however, we want to constrain the type of transformation further. For instance, we might want to assume that the two data sets can be aligned by translation and rotation alone without scaling or reflection. This might be useful if we want to compare shapes that are represented by prominent points on their surface. If the two shapes are similar then there exists a translation and rotation matrix A such that the two point sets match closely. If the shapes are dissimilar there will still be a such a matrix A that describes the best rotational and translational parameters for aligning the two shapes, but the sum of the distances between corresponding points in the two sets will be large. We thus obtain a similarity measure of shapes. In the following we will only consider the three-dimensional case.

The easiest way to constrain the type of matrix we want to allow would be to simply replace the least squares estimation problem of equation 11.3 into a constrained optimization problem where the solution matrix B is required to be orthonormal:

$$BB^t = I,$$

thus guaranteeing that only matrices that represent rotations are obtained. It turns out however, that this is quite an awkward way of handling this problem. In the following, we will therefore present a much better approach. As the proof of its correctness is beyond the scope of this book we will present the technique without proof. A more detailed description can be found in [146], [147].

Representation of rotations

First of all we need to find a convenient way of representing rotations. There are several alternative ways. Rotations can for instance be represented as matrix multiplications where the rotation matrix must be orthonormal, i.e. $BB^t = I$. Secondly, we can identify a rotation axis and a rotation angle. In three dimensions, we need four parameters: three for the rotation axis and one for the rotation angle.

In the following, we will discuss a third option which turns out to be the most useful in our context. The principal idea is to represent rotations in $\mathbf{R}^3$ by an entity called *quaternions* [130, p.1063], [147]. Quaternions are symbols of the form

$$\mathbf{a} = a_0 + a_1\mathbf{i} + a_2\mathbf{j} + a_3\mathbf{k},$$

where

$$\mathbf{i}^2 = \mathbf{j}^2 = \mathbf{k}^2 = -1,$$
$$\mathbf{ij} = \mathbf{k} = -\mathbf{ji},$$
$$\mathbf{jk} = \mathbf{i} = -\mathbf{kj},$$
$$\mathbf{ki} = \mathbf{j} = -\mathbf{ik}.$$

and the $a_i, i = 0, 1, 2, 3$ are real numbers. Multiplications between quaternions follow the distributive rule so that

$$\begin{aligned}
\mathbf{a} \cdot \mathbf{b} = \ &(a_0 b_0 - a_1 b_1 - a_2 b_2 - a_3 b_3) + (a_0 b_1 + a_1 b_0 + a_2 b_3 + a_3 b_2)\mathbf{i} \\
&+ (a_0 b_2 + a_2 b_0 + a_1 b_3 + a_3 b_1)\mathbf{j} + (a_0 b_3 + a_3 b_0 + a_1 b_2 + a_2 b_1)\mathbf{k}.
\end{aligned}$$

Rotations are represented by special types of quaternion which satisfy

$$a_0^2 + a_1^2 + a_2^2 + a_3^2 = 1,$$

i.e. rotations are exactly the *unit quaternions* that may be seen as points on the surface of a unit sphere in $\mathbf{R}^4$.

Rotation by an angle ϕ about a unit vector (v_1, v_2, v_3) is represented by the quaternion

$$\mathbf{a} = \cos(\phi/2) + v_1 \sin(\phi/2)\mathbf{i} + v_2 \sin(\phi/2)\mathbf{j} + v_3 \sin(\phi/2)\mathbf{k}.$$

The corresponding rotation matrix is:

$$R = \begin{bmatrix} a_0^2 + a_1^2 - a_2^2 - a_3^2 & 2(a_1 a_2 - a_0 a_3) & 2(a_1 a_3 + a_0 a_2) \\ 2(a_1 a_2 + a_0 a_3) & a_0^2 + a_2^2 - a_1^2 - a_3^2 & 2(a_2 a_3 + a_0 a_1) \\ 2(a_1 a_3 - a_0 a_2) & 2(a_2 a_3 + a_0 a_1) & a_0^2 + a_3^2 - a_1^2 - a_2^2 \end{bmatrix}.$$

Estimating registration parameters

Using the quaternion representation we need to estimate four rotational parameters and three translational parameters to estimate the displacement between our two point sets. Let us place these parameters into one vector $q = [q_T, q_R]$ where q_T represents the translation vector and q_R the rotation quaternion.

Estimating q consists of minimizing the function

$$f(q) = \frac{1}{n} \sum_{i=0}^{n-1} \|x_i - R(q_R)u_i - q_T\|^2$$

where $R(q_R)$ denotes the rotation matrix corresponding to the quaternion q_R.

The centre of gravity of both point sets is computed as:

$$\mu_x = \frac{1}{n} \sum_{i=0}^{n-1} x_i \quad \text{and} \quad \mu_u = \frac{1}{n} \sum_{i=0}^{n-1} u_i$$

Next, we need the cross-covariance matrix C of the two sets, which is given by:

$$C = \sum_{i=0}^{n-1} (u_i - x_i)(u_i - x_i)^T = \sum_{i=0}^{n-1} u_i x_i - \mu_u \mu_x$$

Let $trace(C)$ denote the trace of C, i.e. the sum of all its diagonal entries, and define a symmetric matrix E as:

$$E = \begin{bmatrix} trace(C) & c_{12} - c_{21} & c_{20} - c_{02} & c_{01} - c_{10} \\ * & 2c_{00} - trace(C) & c_{01} + c_{10} & c_{02} + c_{20} \\ * & * & 2c_{11} - trace(C) & c_{12} + c_{21} \\ * & * & * & 2c_{22} - trace(C) \end{bmatrix}$$

Lastly, we compute the eigenvectors and eigenvalues of matrix E (for instance using Jacobi's method [138]). It turns out that the rotation quaternion that minimizes the goal function 11.3 is the unit eigenvector belonging to the largest eigenvalue of E. Let q_R denote this vector. The optimal translational parameter can then be computed as:

$$q_T = \mu_x - R(q_R)\mu_u.$$

We have thus obtained rigid transformation parameters $[q_T, q_R]$ that optimally align the two points sets.

11.3   The ICP Algorithm

In the previous two sections we learned how to align two sets of points where correspondences between individual points were known. In many instances however, such correspondences are not known. Suppose for example that you have extracted some feature points of some object in one image and you now try to find this same object in a second image that depicts this object in a translated and rotated form. The way to go about solving this problem is to extract salient feature points in both images such as points on an edge, and try to align the feature points from both images. In this case, you will not know which feature point in the first image corresponds to which point in the second image.

In the following, we will introduce the so-called *ICP algorithm* [148] which solves this problem. As before, we denote the two sets of points as U and X

$$U = \{u_i, i = 0, 1, 2, .., n\} \text{ and } X = \{x_i, i = 0, 1, 2, .., k\}.$$

Note that U and X need not have the same number of elements. Without loss of generality we may assume that $k \geq n$. Let us regard X as the "model" shape to which the points of U are to be aligned.

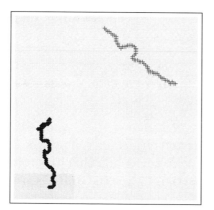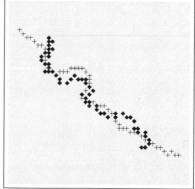

Figure 11.2: Two point sets before and after registration by ICP

The algorithm works in an iterative fashion in which at each iteration the set U is shifted and rotated a little closer towards the model shape. The iteration is initialized by setting $U_0 = U$, and $q_0 = [1,0,0,0,0,0,0]^t$, which corresponds to no translation and no rotation. The following steps are applied until convergence is achieved:

1. Compute the set $Y \subseteq X$ of closest points of U, i.e. for each point in $u \in U$ determine a point $x \in X$ which is closest in distance to u. (Y will have the same number of points as U.)

2. Apply the algorithm of the previous section to obtain a registration vector $q = [q_R, q_T]$ which best aligns Y with U_0.

3. Apply the translation and rotation contained in q to U_0.

4. Compute the mean-squared error.

5. Terminate if this error falls below a predetermined threshold, otherwise go to step 1.

Fortunately, the ICP algorithm is guaranteed to converge to a solution. The reason is that with each step of the iteration the average distance between corresponding points decreases. In addition, by computing the set of closest points better correspondences are generated at each step. A formal proof of the convergence is given in [148].

However, ICP does not always converge to the desired solution, as the algorithm sometimes leads us into a local minimum, i.e. a locally optimal solution that may be quite different from the global minimum. There are several ways to deal with the problem, although none always works. The easiest thing to do is simply to start out with several different starting vectors $[q_t, q_R]$ as the choice of the starting vector determines into which local minimum we are led. So we try out a few candidates – perhaps only computing a few iterations – accept the one that yielded the smallest error and proceed with this vector until convergence is achieved. For further reading on optimization techniques see Press et al. [138].

11.4 Principal axes alignment

The registration methods introduced in the previous sections presuppose that correspondences between individual points in the two point sets must either be given beforehand, or they must be estimated as in

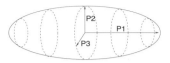

Figure 11.3: Principal axes of an object

the ICP algorithm. Sometimes however, we can use a much simpler approach. The basic idea is to align the two data sets as a whole, viewing them as two "clouds" of points rather than as a collection of individual points.

In other words, we want to align global features extracted from both sets instead of local features such as locations of individual points. Specifically, the features we want to align are the centre of mass and the principal axes. Remember from section 3.3 that the centre of mass as well as the principal axes can be computed from the first- and second-order moments. As a reminder see figure 11.3. The principal axes define an orthogonal coordinate system defined by the eigenvectors of the inertia matrix.

Therefore, the process of registering two sets of points using the principal axes method consists in the following steps:

- determining the centre of mass μ_1 and μ_2 of both sets;

- shifting both sets so that their centres of mass reside in the origin of the coordinate system;

- computing the inertia matrix and the principal axes of both point sets;

- rotating one data set into the other so that their principal axes point into the same directions.

In addition to its simplicity, this algorithm has the advantage that it works for various kinds of input representation. For instance, in addition to sets of points, binary raster images or even boundary representations may be used because moments are defined for all three forms of representation.

Its disadvantage though is that it may produce quite inexact results. This is especially true when the shape is almost spherical so that small perturbations due to noise may lead to a completely different orientation of the principal axes. Therefore, the principal axes registration method is often used only as a first step after which more refined methods follow.

11.5 Aligning volumetric images

Let us now come to the more difficult problem of registering entire volumes. Imagine two volume data sets are given and we want to align them geometrically so that they overlap as closely as possible.

In the previous sections we have discussed methods of registering sets of points or binary raster images. These methods do not make use of the grey values in the image. This may be quite disadvantageous as grey values may serve as an important clue in the registration problem.

The most straightforward approach is to compute the similarity between the two volumetric images at various degrees of rotation and translation trying to find the best match. Quite often, correlation coefficients are used as a similarity metric. Alternatively, an information theoretic measure called *mutual information* may be used instead [149].

Sometimes however, global affine linear transformations are not sufficient to describe the disparity between the two images.

Therefore, instead of using global affine transformations, we must revert to local and non-linear methods. The way to go about this is the following: we subdivide one image into several small subimages and search for optimal matching positions for each subimage. This gives different parameters for each subimage so that in order to obtain a suitable registration of the entire image intermediate values must be interpolated. Clearly, this involves a lot of computational effort. However, the results are usually more accurate.

11.6 Aligning segmented structures

So far, we have discussed techniques for registering point sets and raster images. Another set of methods aims at aligning structures that have been extracted from the two images by some segmentation routine. Surfaces, lines or some segmented volumetric structures may be used for this purpose. In all cases, we assume that such structures have been detected in both images, and we now need to find correspondences be-

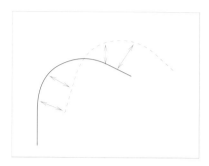

Figure 11.4: Distances between structures

tween them. As with point set matching, we must solve an optimization problem which yields the best geometric transformation that aligns the given structures.

Figure 11.4 illustrates the problem: we must find a transformation that minimizes the overall distance between the structures. Remember from section 4.3 that the distance transform of a binary image contains the distance at each point towards the nearest foreground voxel. In the present application, we define as foreground all voxels belonging to a structure in one image, and compute its distance transform. We then project the foreground voxels of the second image into the distance transformed image and sum up all distance values along the projected foreground voxels. This sum gives an estimate of the overall disparity between the two structures. A large value indicates a large disparity, and a small value indicates a close match. Clearly, the registration problem can now be reformulated as a minimization problem where the goal function is given by the sum of the distance values.

Various approaches to solving this optimization problem have been proposed. Staib et al. [150], for instance, use a genetic search algorithm. Hill et al. [143] additionally incorporate other sources of information to ensure a more robust result.

Appendix A

Displaying volumetric images

There are three basically different approaches to displaying volumetric images which may be called *volume slicing*, *surface rendering* and *volume rendering*. In the following, we will briefly introduce each of these three techniques. However, we will not attempt to present a complete overview of all available visualization techniques. The purpose of this presentation is to give a very brief introduction into the basic concepts so that the process by which some of the images presented in this book were generated becomes comprehensible.

A.1 Volume slicing

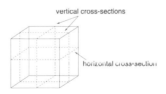

Figure A.1: Three orthogonal sections through a volume

In volume slicing, we present the image as a series of slices which represent sections through the volume. These sections may have any conceivable orientation with respect to the voxel grid. However, mostly sections which are aligned with the voxel grid are used. Figure A.1

shows three such orthogonal sections through a volume. We have already used this technique in previous chapters to visualize the effect of image processing in all three spatial dimensions.

A more difficult problem arises when the section to be visualized – usually also called the *viewing plane* – is not aligned with the voxel grid as illustrated in figure A.2. In order to prepare the viewing plane for visualization, it must be converted into a two-dimensional raster matrix – called the *frame buffer* – containing the pixels to be displayed on a computer screen. If the viewing plane is not aligned with the voxel grid, its display matrix must be filled using interpolated values. We may for instance use trilinear interpolation as introduced in section 6.1 for that purpose. A sophisticated method for specifying arbitrary cutting planes through a volume is described in [151].

A.2   Surface rendering

In surface rendering, we first segment the image to determine the objects it shows. We then extract the object's surfaces using any of the surface tiling techniques discussed in chapter 9. And finally, the resulting surface is displayed using rendering techniques to be discussed in the following.

Displaying a three-dimensional object on a two-dimensional computer screen involves solving several problems and making modelling decisions. Firstly, we must decide on a viewing direction and the position of the observer relative to the object. Secondly, we must decide on a projection model which describes the way in which the object is

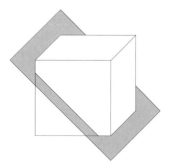

Figure A.2: A diagonal viewing plane

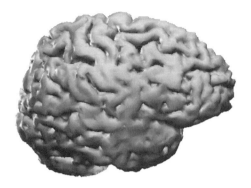

Figure A.3: A surface rendering

projected onto the screen. And thirdly, we must choose an appropriate illumination and shading model determined by the properties of a set of light sources together with the characteristics of the object's surface. In the following, we will briefly discuss all three topics. For more information see for instance [130], [152], [153], [154].

A.2.1 Illumination and shading

Let us begin with illumination and shading models. The simplest assumption to make with respect to illumination is that there are no direct light sources so that only background light – called *ambient light* – is present. In this case, each point on the surface is illuminated equally and its appearance is only determined by the overall intensity of the ambient light and by the surface properties.

Let I_a denote the intensity of the ambient light, and k_a the object's intrinsic surface intensity. Then the intensity at any surface point visible on the screen is given by [130, p.723]:

$$I_1 = I_a \, k_a.$$

The above model is rather crude and seldom produces satisfactory results. To improve it, let us incorporate a source of light into the model. We assume that there is only one source of light and it radiates equally in all directions from a predetermined point in space. Then, using Lambert's law, the intensity at each point on the viewing plane is determined

light source

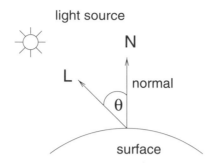

Figure A.4: Lambertian reflection

by:

$$I_2 = \begin{cases} I_L \, \cos(\theta) k_d, & \text{if } 0 \leq \theta \leq \pi/2 \\ 0, & \text{otherwise} \end{cases}$$

where $0 \leq k_d \leq 1$ denotes the diffuse reflection coefficient, I_L is the intensity of the light source, and θ is the angle between the surface normal N and the vector L which points in the direction of the light source (see figure A.4). This model is usually called *diffuse reflection* or *Lambertian reflection.*

While Lambertian reflection is a definite improvement over our first model, it does not take the observer's position into account, so it is still not a realistic model. Another more complete model called *specular reflection* allows us to model shiny, specular surfaces. Note that highlights on a shiny surface are viewer dependent: as the viewer's position changes the highlight seems to move along the object's surface. Figure A.5 shows the various parameters required for this model: in addition to the light source vector L and surface normal N, we also need a vector A pointing in the direction of the viewer, and a vector R representing the direction of reflection. If the angle α between R and A is zero, then the viewer sees a maximally reflected light, provided the surface is shiny. The angle α determines the broadness of the highlight. In specular reflection, this term is modelled by the term

$$\cos^c(\alpha)$$

where c is called the *specular-reflection exponent.* A high value of c entails a small focused highlight, a small value of c leads to a broad, unfocused highlight. Together with the intensity of the light source I_L,

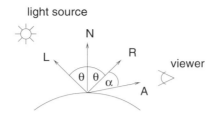

Figure A.5: Specular reflection

and the specular reflection coefficient k_s, the specular reflection model is given by:

$$I_3 = \begin{cases} I_L \cos^c(\alpha) \, k_s, & \text{if } 0 \le \alpha \le \pi/2 \\ 0, & \text{otherwise.} \end{cases}$$

Generally, all three models discussed so far are combined into one, so that ambient, diffuse and specular reflection together determine the appearance of a scene. The combined model is given by:

$$I = I_1 + I_2 + I_3.$$

So far, we have discussed reflection at a single point on a surface. To obtain shading models for entire surface patches, various interpolation schemes are used, which we will not present here.

A.2.2 Projection models

Projection models describe a transform that projects a three-dimensional object onto a two-dimensional viewing plane. Usually, projection models define a *centre of projection* from which projection rays emanate towards the object while intersecting the viewing plane. The projection centre coincides with the position of the observer.

There are two basic projection models to choose from: parallel projection and central projection (see figure A.6). In *central projection*, the projection rays start from one projection centre and fan out towards the object as illustrated in figure A.6a. In *parallel projection* (figure A.6b), we assume that the centre of projection is at infinity so that the projection rays are parallel. In most applications, central projection is the preferred method of choice.

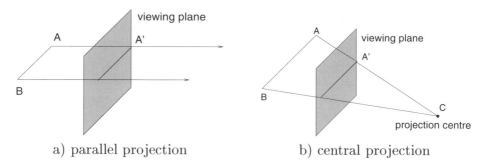

a) parallel projection   b) central projection

Figure A.6: Projection models

A.2.3 Visible surface determination

Once the projection model is chosen, we must determine which portions of the object are visible from the viewer's perspective and fall into the viewing plane. As the viewing plane is of course finite, some parts of the scene may be outside the range of the viewing plane or hidden from view. The viewing plane is represented by the two-dimensional display matrix, the *frame buffer*, while the object is given in a boundary representation, usually given as a set of facets.

In order to display facets in a frame buffer, they must be *scan-converted* so that each facet is represented by a number of points in the frame buffer. See [155] for further reading about scan-conversion.

There are a number of algorithms for visible surface determination of which we will present just two: the *Z-buffer algorithm* and the *ray-casting method*.

Z-Buffer

In Z-buffer rendering, we need a new data structure – the *Z-buffer* – in addition to the frame buffer. The Z-buffer has the same number of rows and columns as the frame buffer. However, it often requires more storage space per pixel than the frame buffer to allow for higher precision. Its prime purpose is to record the distance between each point of the viewing plane and the corresponding surface facet. The values in the Z-buffer are continually updated throughout the process.

In the first step, the Z-buffer is initialized to some large distance value, which should exceed the largest distance from any facet towards the viewer. Subsequently, each facet of the surface is projected onto

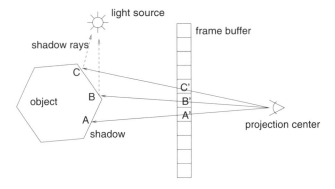

Figure A.7: Ray casting

the viewing plane and scan-converted into the frame buffer. For each scan-converted point we determine the distance between its location on the viewing plane and that on the object's surface. If this distance is less than the current value in the Z-buffer, we update the Z-buffer at this point and write its intensity computed from the given illumination and shading model into the frame buffer. This procedure is repeated for each surface primitive.

Note that the procedure for updating the Z-buffer prevents facets that are occluded by other facets to be displayed in the frame buffer. At some step in the process, they will be overwritten by other facets that are closer to the viewer.

Ray casting

Ray casting – sometimes also referred to as *ray tracing* – is a more elaborate rendering method. It usually produces more realistic results but also requires more computation time. Its basic principle is simple: starting at the viewer's eye (the projection centre), a ray is cast through each point in the frame buffer onto the scene as illustrated in figure A.7.

If the frame buffer has n_r rows and n_c columns then there will be $n_r \times n_c$ such rays. For each ray, we determine whether it intersects an object in the scene. It it does, we compute its illumination and shading value and write it into the frame buffer at the corresponding location. In figure A.7, there are three intersection points – A, B, and C – whose projections in the frame buffer are A', B', and C'. Note that point A is in the shadow so it will not be visible even though it is not occluded.

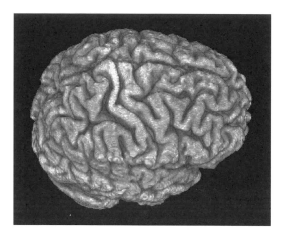

Figure A.8: A volume rendered image

To determine shadows, a second type of rays – called *shadow rays* –
are projected from the point of intersection towards the light source. If
the shadow ray hits a surface on its way to the light source, then the
intersection point is not illuminated and must be in the shadow.

In ray tracing, we follow a ray's fate even further. If a ray hits
a surface it may be reflected if the surface is specular or it may be
refracted if the surface is transparent. Sometimes, both refraction and
reflection occur at the same time. In any case, the initial ray may
be split into several subrays which in turn may hit other surfaces, split
again and so on. Thus, ray tracing consists in recursively following each
ray and all its child rays until they either meet a non-reflective and non-
refractive surface or do not intersect any more surfaces. Clearly, this
procedure may be extremely time-consuming, especially if we try to
follow each ray to its very end.

A.3   Volume rendering

Volume rendering differs from surface rendering in that it does not
require a boundary representation of the objects to be displayed. In
fact, volume rendering directly renders the raster image without any
intermediate data structure. This is indeed its prime advantage in our
context. Our primary data structure is the volumetric raster image
so that volume rendering spares us the trouble of computing a surface

representation which may be difficult to obtain. Again, we will only give a very brief introduction. For further reading see for instance [156].

A.3.1 Illumination and shading

As before, we need to establish a shading and illumination model to determine the rendering process. While essentially the same principles as for surface rendering hold, there are two additional points to consider. Firstly, remember that for the shading model we need to determine surface normals.

If the volumetric image to be rendered is not segmented, then we do not know where the surfaces are and hence we do not have any access to surface normals. However, we can of course still determine grey value gradients using any of the edge detection techniques discussed in chapter 7. Even if the image is segmented, these same techniques can still be applied. In addition, there are some specific techniques for determining surface normals of segmented images (see for instance Yagel et al. [157]).

The second point to consider is the following. If the image is not segmented and contains a whole range of grey values then we may attribute a *transparency value* to each grey value, these are best stored in a look-up table. As a result, certain grey value ranges may be made to appear transparent or hazy and others oblique, so that objects which are characterized by grey value ranges are emphasized and others are suppressed from view.

A.3.2 Discrete ray casting

The most popular volume rendering method is called *discrete ray casting*. It is very similar to the continuous ray casting method of section A.2.3. The basic difference is that instead of using continuous rays we now use discrete rays which are cast into a discrete raster image rather than into a continuous scene.

Discrete rays are obtained by transforming the continuous line representing the original ray into an n-connected path (see section 2.1) such that each voxel which is intersected by the continuous line is added to the resulting n-path. If 26-adjacency is used, fewer voxels are generated than in the 6-adjacency case. However, a 26-adjacent path may fail to detect thin surfaces. Figure A.9 illustrates this problem: object A is

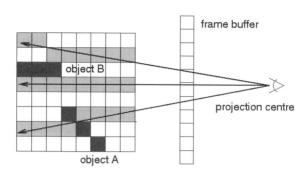

Figure A.9: Problems in discrete ray casting (discrete rays are shown in light grey, object voxels in black)

not intersected by the 26-path representing one of the discrete rays, and will therefore not be projected onto the frame buffer. Note that a 6-path would work correctly here.

Another problem may arise due to the fact that in central projection rays fan out so that portions of the image which are far away from the centre of projection are not as densely covered by the discrete rays as the front image portions. As a result, far away objects may be missed altogether. Object B in figure A.9 is an example of this problem.

Both problems can be alleviated by *supersampling*, i.e. by increasing the number of rays to be cast through each pixel in the frame buffer. Figure A.8 shows a volume rendered image of a human brain extracted from a magnetic resonance image (see also section 8.3).

References

[1] A. Rosenfeld, A. Kak. *Digital Picture Processing*, volume Vol. I/II. Academic Press, San Diego, CA, 2nd edition, 1982.

[2] D.H. Ballard, C.M. Brown. *Computer Vision*. Prentice Hall, Inc., Englewood Cliffs, NJ, 1982.

[3] A.K. Jain. *Fundamentals of digital image processing*. Prentice Hall, Englewood Cliffs, NJ, 1989.

[4] R.M. Haralick, L.G. Shapiro. *Computer and Robot Vision, Volume 1*. Addison-Wesley, Reading, MA, 1992.

[5] N. Ayache. Medical computer vision, virtual reality and robotics. *Image and Vision Computing*, 13(4):295–313, 1995.

[6] T.Y. Kong, A. Rosenfeld. Digital topology: introduction and survey. *Computer Vision, Graphics, and Image Processing*, 48:357–393, 1989.

[7] K. Voss. *Discrete Images, Objects, and Functions in Zn*. Springer Verlag, Berlin, Heidelberg, New York, 1993.

[8] T.Y.Kong, A.W. Roscoe. Continuous analogs of axiomatized digital surfaces. *Computer Vision, Graphics, and Image Processing*, 29:60–86, 1985.

[9] D.G. Morgenthaler, A. Rosenfeld. Surfaces in three-dimensional digital images. *Inform. and Control*, 51:227–247, 1981.

[10] G.M. Reed. On the characterization of simple closed surfaces in three-dimensional digital images. *Computer Vision, Graphics, and Image Processing*, 25:226–235, 1984.

[11] V.A. Kovalevsky. Finite topology as applied to image analysis. *Computer Vision, Graphics, and Image Processing*, 46:141–161, 1989.

[12] A. Pope, D. Lowe. Vista: A software environment for computer vision research. In *IEEE Computer Society Conference on Computer Vision and Pattern –Recognition (CVPR)*, Seattle, WA, 1994.

[13] R. Lumia. A new three-dimensional connected components algorithm. *Computer Vision, Graphics, and Image Processing*, 23:207–217, 1983.

[14] L. Thurfjell, E. Bengtsson, B. Nordin. A new three-dimensional connected components labeling algorithm with simultaneous object feature extraction capability. *Computer Vision, Graphics, and Image Processing*, 54(4):357–364, 1992.

[15] L. Thurfjell, E. Bengtsson, B, Nordin. A boundary approach for fast neighbourhood operations on three-dimensional binary data. *Graphical Models and Image Processing*, 57(1):13–19, 1995.

[16] M.B. Dillencourt, H. Samet, M. Tamminen. A general approach to connected-component labelling for arbitrary image representations. *Journal of the ACM*, 39(2):253–280, 1992.

[17] H. Samet, M. Tamminen. An improved approach to connected component labelling of images. In *IEEE Computer Society Conference on Computer Vision and Pattern –Recognition (CVPR)*, pages 312–318, Miami Beach, Fla., 1986. IEEE.

[18] A.V. Aho, J.D. Ullman. *Foundations of Computer Science*. Computer Science Press, W.H. Freeman and Company, New York, 1995.

[19] C. Montani, R. Scopigno. Rendering volumetric data using the STICKS representation scheme. In *Computer Graphics (San Diego Workshop on Volume Visualization)*, volume 24, pages 87–93, November 1990.

[20] I. Gargantini. Linear octrees for fast processing of three-dimensional objects. *Computer Graphics and Image Processing*, 20:365–374, 1982.

[21] C.A. Shaffer, H.Samet. Optimal quadtree contruction algorithms. *Computer Vision, Graphics, and Image Processing*, 37:402–419, 1987.

[22] H.H. Chen, T.S. Huang. A survey of construction and manipulation of octrees. *Computer Vision, Graphics, and Image Processing*, 43:409–431, 1988.

[23] G.M. Morton. A computer oriented geodetic data base and a new technique in file sequencing. IBM, Ltd., Ottawa, Canada, 1966.

[24] R. Shu, M.S. Kankanhalli. Efficient linear octree generation from voxels. *Image and Vision Computing*, 12(5):297–303, 1994.

[25] F.C. Holroyd, D.C. Mason. Efficient linear octree generation from voxels. *Image and Vision Computing*, 8(3):218–224, 1990.

[26] H. Samet. Neighbor finding in images represented by octrees. *Computer Vision, Graphics, and Image Processing*, 46(3):367–386, 1989.

[27] C.-N. Lee, T. Poston, A. Rosenfeld. Holes and genus of 2D and 3D digital images. *Computer Vision, Graphics, and Image Processing: Graphical Models and Image Processing*, 55(1):20–47, 1993.

[28] S.N. Srihari. Representation of three-dimensional digital images. *ACM Computing Surveys*, 13(4):399–424, 1981.

[29] C.N. Lee, A. Rosenfeld. Computing the Euler number of a 3D image. In *Proc. of IEEE Conference on Computer Vision*, pages 567–571, London, 1987.

[30] C.-N. Lee, T. Poston. Winding and Euler numbers for 2D and 3D digital images. *Computer Vision, Graphics, and Image Processing: Graphical Models and Image Processing*, 53(6):522–537, 1991.

[31] D. Hilbert, S. Cohn-Vossen. *Anschauliche Geometrie*. Springer-Verlag, Berlin, 1932.

[32] C.M. Park, A. Rosenfeld. Connectivity and genus in three dimensions. Technical Report TR-156, Computer Science Center, University of Maryland, College Park, MD, 1971.

[33] S. Lobregt, P.W. Verbeek, F.C.A. Groen. Three-dimensional skeletonization, principle, and algorithm. *IEEE Transactions on Pattern Analysis and Machine Intelligence*, 2:75–77, 1980.

[34] D.G. Morgenthaler. Three-dimensional digital topology: the genus. Technical Report TR-980, Computer Science Center, Univ. of Maryland, College Park, MD, 1980.

[35] D.C. Hogg. Shape in machine vision. *Image and Vision Computing*, 11(6):309–316, 1993.

[36] J.J. Koenderink. *Solid Shape*. The MIT Press, Cambridge, MA, 1990.

[37] T.L. Faber, E.M. Stokely. Orientation of 3-D structures in medical images. *IEEE Transactions on Pattern Analysis and Machine Intelligence*, 10(5):626–632, 1988.

[38] J.M. Galvez, M. Canton. Normalization and shape recognition of three-dimensional objects by 3D moments. *Pattern Recognition Letters*, 26(5):667–681, 1993.

[39] F.A. Sadjadi E.L. Hall. Three-dimensional moment invariants. *IEEE Transactions on Pattern Analysis and Machine Intelligence*, 2(2):127–135, 1980.

[40] Chong-Huah Lo, Hon-Son Don. 3-D moments forms: their constructon and application to object identification and positioning. *IEEE Transactions on Pattern Analysis and Machine Intelligence*, 11(10):1053–1064, 1989.

[41] P.K. Saha, B.B. Chauduri. 3D digital topology under binary transformation with applications. *Computer Vision, Graphics, and Image Processing: Image Inderstanding*, 63(3):418–429, 1996.

[42] G. Malandain, G. Bertrand and N. Ayache. Topological segmentation of discrete surfaces. *International Journal of Computer Vision*, 10(2):183–197, 1993.

[43] Y.F. Tsao, K.S. Fu. A parallel thinning algorithm for 3D pictures. *Computer Graphics Image Processing*, 17:315–331, 1981.

[44] G. Bertrand, G. Malandain. A new characterization of three-dimensional simple points. *Pattern Recognition Letters*, 15:169–175, 1994.

[45] P.K. Saha, B.B. Chaudhuri, B. Chanda, D.Dutta Majumder. Topology preservation in 3D digital space. *Pattern Recognition*, 27(2):295–300, 1994.

[46] G. Malandain, G. Bertrand. Fast characterization of 3D simple points. In *International Conference on Pattern Recognition*, The Hague, Netherlands, 1990.

[47] S.N. Srihari, J.K. Udupa, M. Yau. Understanding the bin of parts. In *Proc. Int. Conf. on Cybernetics and Society*, pages 44 49, Denver, CO, 1979.

[48] Y.F. Tsao, K.S. Fu. A 3D parallel skeletonwise thinning algorithm. In *IEEE Pattern Recognition and Image Proc. Conf.*, pages 678–683, 1982.

[49] W.X. Gong, G. Bertrand. A simple parallelel 3D thinning algorithm. In *International Conference on Pattern Recognition*, pages 188–190, 1990.

[50] C. Min Ma, M. Sonka. A fully parallel 3D thinning algorithm and its application. *Computer Vision, Graphics, and Image Processing: Image Inderstanding*, 64(3):420–433, 1996.

[51] Seung-Cheol Goh, Chung-Nim Lee. Counting minimal paths in 3D digital geometry. *Pattern Recognition Letters*, Nov 1992.

[52] G. Borgefors. Distance transformations in digital images. *Computer Vision, Graphics, and Image Processing*, 34:344–371, 1986.

[53] G. Borgefors. Distance transforms in arbitrary dimensions. *Computer Vision, Graphics, and Image Processing*, 27:321–345, 1984.

[54] A.L.D. Beckers, A.W.M. Smeulders. Optimization of length measurements for isotropic distance transformations in three dimensions. *Computer Vision, Graphics, and Image Processing: Image Inderstanding*, 55(3):296–306, 1992.

[55] N. Kiryati, G. Szekely. Estimating shortest paths and minimal distances on digitized three-dimensional surfaces. *Pattern Recognition*, 26(11):1623–1637, 1993.

[56] B.J.H. Verwer. Local distances for distance transformations in two and three dimensions. *Pattern Recognition Letters*, 12:671–682, 1991.

[57] G. Borgefors. On digital distance transformations in three dimensions. *Computer Vision, Graphics, and Image Processing: Image Inderstanding*, 64(3):368–376, 1996.

[58] T. Saito, J.-I. Toriwaki. New algorithms for euclidean distance transformation of an n-dimensional digitized picture with applications. *Pattern Recognition*, 27(11):1551–1565, 1994.

[59] P.E. Danielsson. Euclidean distance mapping. *Computer Graphics and Image Processing*, 14:227–248, 1980.

[60] I. Ragnemalm. The euclidean distance transform in arbitrary dimensions. *Pattern Recognition Letters*, 14:883–888, 1993.

[61] C. Arcelli, G. Sanniti di Baja. Ridge points in euclidean distance maps. *Pattern Recognition Letters*, 13:237–243, 1992.

[62] C. Arcelli, G. Sanniti di Baja. Euclidean skeleton via centre-of-maximal-disc extraction. *Image and Vision Computing*, 11(3):163–173, 1993.

[63] C.W. Niblack, P.B. Gibbons, D.W.Capson. Generating skeletons and centerlines from the distance transform. *Computer Vision, Graphics, and Image Processing*, 54(5):420–437, 1992.

[64] G. Malandain, S. Fernández-Vidal. Topologically correct skeleton in n-D. In *5th conf. discrete geometry for computer imagery*, Clermont-Ferrand, France, Sept. 1995.

[65] J.A. Goldak, X. Yu, A. Knight, L. Dong. Constructing discrete medial axis of 3-D objects. *Internat. J. Comput. Geom. Appl.*, 1(3):327–339, 1991.

[66] H. Blum. A transformation for extracting new descriptors of shape. In *Models for the Perception of Speech and visual form.* MIT Press, Cambridge, MA, 1967.

[67] J.W. Brandt. Describing a solid with the three-dimensional skeleton. *spie*, Vol. 1830, Curves and Surfaces in Computer Vision and Graphics III:258–269, 1992.

[68] R.L. Ogniewicz, M. Ilg. Voronoi skeletons: theory and applications. In *Proc. Computer Vision and Pattern Recognition (CVPR 92)*, pages 63–69. Computer Society Press, 1992.

[69] M. Näf, O. Kübler, R. Kikinis, G, Székely. Characterization and recognition of 3D organ shape in medical image analysis using skeletonization. In *Proc. Mathematical Methods in Biomedical Image Analysis*, pages 139–150, San Francisco, CA, June 1996. IEEE Computer Society.

[70] J.D. Furst, S.M. Pizer, D.H. Eberly. Marching cores: a method for extracting cores from 3D medical images. In *Proc. Mathematical Methods in Biomedical Image Analysis*, pages 124–130, San Francisco, CA, June 1996. IEEE Computer Society.

[71] J. Serra. *Image Analysis and Mathematical Morphology.* Academic Press, San Diego, CA, 1982.

[72] G. Matheron. *Random Sets and Integal Geometry.* Wiley, New York,NY, 1975.

[73] P. Maragos, R.W. Schafer. Morphological systems for multidimensional signal processing. *Proceedings of the IEEE*, 78(4):690–710, 1990.

[74] S.S. Biswas, A.K. Ray. Region merging in 3-D images using morpholopical operators. *Pattern Recognition Letters*, 14:23–30, 1993.

[75] R.S. Acharya, R. Laurette. Mathematical morphology for 3d image analysis. In *Intern. Conf. on Acoustics, Speech and Signal Proc. (ICASSP)*, New York, 1988.

[76] K. Preston. Three-dimensional mathematical morphology. *Image and Vision Computing*, 9:285–295, 1991.

[77] R. Bracewell. *Tne Fourier transform and its applications.* McGraw-Hill, New York, NY, 1965.

[78] B. Jähne. *Digitale Bildverarbeitung.* Springer-Verlag, Berlin, Heidelberg, 3rd edition, 1993.

[79] J.W. Tukey. *Exploratory Data Analysis.* Addison Wesley, Menlo Park, CA, 1971.

[80] J.S. Lee. Digital image smoothing and the sigma filter. *Computer Vision, Graphics, and Image Processing*, 24:255–269, 1983.

[81] P. Perona, J. Malik. Scale-space and edge detection using anisotropic diffusion. *IEEE Transactions on Pattern Analysis and Machine Intelligence*, 12(7):629–639, 1990.

[82] G. Gerig, O. Kübler, R. Kikinis, F. Jolesz. Nonlinear anisotropic filtering of MRI data. *IEEE Transactions on Medical Imaging*, 11(2):221–232, 1992.

[83] C.R. Appledorn. A new approach to the interpolation of sampled data. *IEEE Transactions on Medical Imaging*, 15(3):369–376, 1996.

[84] A. Goshtasby, D.A. Turner, L.V. Ackerman. Matching tomographic slices for interpolation. *IEEE Transactions on Medical Imaging*, 11(4):507–516, 1992.

[85] S.P. Raya, J.K. Udupa. Shape-based interpolation of multidimensional objects. *IEEE Transactions on Medical Imaging*, 9(1):32–42, 1990.

[86] G.J. Grevera, J.K. Udupa. Shape-based interpolation of multidimensional grey-level images. *IEEE Transactions on Medical Imaging*, 15(6):881–892, 1996.

[87] J. Prewitt. Picture processing and psychophysics. In B. Lipkin and A. Rosenfeld, editor, *Object Enhancement and Extraction*, pages 75–149. Academic Press, New York, NY, 1970.

[88] Y.J. Zhang. Quantative study of 3D gradient operators. *Image and Vision Computing*, 11(10), 1993.

[89] S.W. Zucker, R.A. Hummel. A three dimensional edge operator. *IEEE Transactions on Pattern Analysis and Machine Intelligence*, 3(3):324–331, 1981.

[90] E.C. Hildreth. The detection of intensity changes by computer and biological vision systems. *Computer Vision, Graphics, and Image Processing*, 22:1–27, 1983.

[91] M. Bomans, K.-H. Höhne, U. Tiede, M. Riemer. 3D segmentation of MR images of the head for 3D display. *IEEE Transactions on Medical Imaging*, 9(2):177–183, 1990.

[92] J. Canny. A computational approach to edge detection. *IEEE Transactions on Pattern Analysis and Machine Intelligence*, 8(6):679–698, 1986.

[93] R. Deriche. Using Canny's criteria to derive a recursively implemented optimal edge detector. *Image and Vision Computing*, 1(2):167–187, 1987.

[94] R. Deriche. Fast algorithms for low level vision. *IEEE Transactions on Pattern Analysis and Machine Intelligence*, 12(1):78–87, 1990.

[95] O. Monga, R. Deriche, J.M. Rocchisani. 3D edge detection using recursive filtering. *Computer Vision, Graphics, and Image Processing*, 53(1):76–87, 1991.

[96] M.P. do Carmo. *Differential Geometry of Curves and Surfaces*. Prentice-Hall, Englewood Cliffs, NJ, 1976.

[97] J.P. Thirion, A. Gourdon. The marching lines algorithm: new results and proofs. Technical Report 1881-1, Institut National de Recherche en Informatique et an Automatique (INRIA), Epidaure, Sophia-Antipolis, France, Apr. 1993.

[98] P. Besl, R. Jain. Intrinsic and extrinsic surface characteristics. In *IEEE Computer Society Conference on Computer Vision and Pattern -Recognition (CVPR)*, pages 226–233, 1985.

[99] E.M. Stokely, S.Y. Wu. Surface parameterization and curvature measurement. *IEEE Transactions on Pattern Analysis and Machine Intelligence*, 14(8):pp.833–840, 1992.

[100] P. Sander. Generic curvature features from 3D images. *IEEE Transactions on Systems, Man, and Cybernetics*, November 1989.

[101] P. Sander, S.W. Zucker. Inferring surface trace and differential structure from 3D images. *IEEE Transactions on Pattern Analysis and Machine Intelligence*, 12(9), 1990.

[102] O. Monga, S. Benayoun. Using partial derivatives of 3D images to extract typical surface features. *Computer Vision and Image Understanding*, 61(2):171–189, 1995.

[103] G.H. Ball, D.J. Hall. Isodata: a novel method of data analysis and pattern classification. In *Intern. Communications Conference*, Philadeplphia, PA, June 1966.

[104] J.C. Bezdek. A convergence theorem for the fuzzy isodata clustering algorithms. *IEEE Transactions on Pattern Analysis and Machine Intelligence*, 2(1):1–8, 1980.

[105] G. Gerig, J. Martin, R. Kikinis, O, Kübler, M. Shenton, F.A. Jolesz. Unsupervised tissue type segmentation of 3D dual-echo MR head data. *Image and Vision Computing*, 10(6):349 ff., 1992.

[106] K. Fukunaga. *Introduction to statistical pattern recognition*. Academic Press, San Diego, CA, 1990.

[107] M. Joliot, B.M. Mazoyer. Three-dimensional segmentation and interpolation of magnetic resonance brain images. *IEEE Transactions on Medical Imaging*, 12(2):269–277, 1993.

[108] K. C. Strasters, J. J. Gerbrands. Three-dimensional image segmentation using split, merge and group approach. *Pattern Recognition Letters*, 12(5):307–325, 1991.

[109] M. Bomans, K.-H. Höhne, U. Tiede, M. Riemer. 3D segmentation of MR images of the head for 3-D display. *IEEE Transactions on Medical Imaging*, 9(2):177–183, 1990.

[110] J. Yia-Jaaski, O. Kübler. Segmentation and analysis of 3D volume images. In *Ninth International Conference on Pattern Recognition (Rome, Italy, November 14–17, 1988)*, pages 951–953, Washington, DC, 1988. Computer Society Press.

[111] Shih-Ping Liou, R.C. Jain. An approach to three dimensional image segmentation. *Computer Vision, Graphics, and Image Processing: Image Inderstanding*, 53(3):237–252, 1991.

[112] S. Geman, D. Geman. Stochastic relaxation, gibbs distributions, and the bayesian restoration of images. *IEEE Transactions on Pattern Analysis and Machine Intelligence*, 6:721–741, 1984.

[113] R. Chellappa, A. Jain (Eds.). *Markov random fields*. Academic Press, San Diego, CA, 1991.

[114] W. M. Wells III , W. E. L. Grimson, R. Kikinis, F. A. Jolesz. Adaptive segmentation of MRI data. In Nicholas Ayache, editor, *Computer Vision, Virtual Reality and Robotics in Medicine*, Lecture Notes in Computer Science. Springer-Verlag, April 1995. ISBN 3-540-59120-6.

[115] F. Kruggel, G.Lohmann. Automatical adaption of the stereotactical coordinate system in brain MRI datasets. In J. Duncan, editor, *15th Intern. Conf. on Information Processing in Medical Imaging*, Poultney, VT, June 1997.

[116] M.E. Brummer, R.M. Mersereau, R.L. Eisner, R.J. Lewine. Automatic detection of brain contours in MRI data sets. *IEEE Transactions on Medical Imaging*, 12(2):153ff., 1993.

[117] E. Artzy, G. Frieder, G.T. Herman. The theory, design, implementation, and evualation of a three-dimensional surface detection algorithm. *Computer Graphics and Image Processing*, 15:1–24, 1981.

[118] A. Rosenfeld. Digital surfaces. *Computer Vision, Graphics, and Image Processing: Graphical Models and Image Processing*, 53(4):305–312, 1991.

[119] J.K. Udupa. Multidimensional digital boundaries. *Computer Vision, Graphics, and Image Processing: Graphical Models and Image Processing*, 56(4):311–323, 1994.

[120] W.E. Lorensen, H.E. Cline. Marching cubes: a high resolution 3D surface construction algorithm. *Computer Graphics*, 21:163–169, 1987.

[121] A. Gueziec, R. Hummel. The wrapper algorithm: surface extraction and simplification. In *IEEE workshop on biomedical image analysis*, San Francisco, CA, June 1994.

[122] D. Meyers, S. Skinner, K. Sloan. Surfaces from contours. *ACM Transactions on Graphics*, 11(3), 1992.

[123] J.D. Boissonnat. Shape reconstruction from planar cross sections. *Computer Vision, Graphics, and Image Processing*, 44(1):1–29, 1988.

[124] J. O'Rourke. *Computational geometry in C*. Cambridge University Press, Cambridge, UK, 1993.

[125] W.J. Schroeder, J.A. Zarge, W.E. Lorensen. Decimation of triangle meshes. *Computer Graphics*, 26(2):65–70, 1992.

[126] H. Hoppe, T. DeRose, T. Duchamp, J. McDonald, W. Stuetzle. Mesh optimization. In James T. Kajiya, editor, *Computer Graphics (SIGGRAPH '93 Proceedings)*, volume 27, pages 19–26, August 1993.

[127] A. Goshtasby. Design and recovery of 2-D and 3-D shapes using rational gaussian curves and surfaces. *International Journal of Computer Vision*, 10(3):233–256, 1993.

[128] P. Sander, S.W. Zucker. Singularities of principal direction fields from 3-D images. *IEEE Transactions on Pattern Analysis and Machine Intelligence*, 14(3), 1992.

[129] P.J. Besl. Geometric modeling and computer vision. *Proc. of the IEEE*, 76(8):936–955, 1988.

[130] J.D. Foley, A. van Damm, S.K. Feiner, J.F. Hughes. *Computer Graphics – Principles and practice*. Addison Wesley Publ., Reading, MA, 1990.

[131] F. Bookstein. *Morphometric tools for landmark data*. Cambridge University Press, Cambridge, UK, 1991.

[132] R. Bolle, B. Vemuri. On three-dimensional surface reconstruction methods. *IEEE Transactions on Pattern Analysis and Machine Intelligence*, 13(1):pp.1–13, 1991.

[133] B. Cernuschi-Frias. *Orientation and location parameter estimation of quadric surfaces in 3-D from a sequence of images*. PhD thesis, Brown Univ., Div. of Engineering, Providence, RI, May 1984.

[134] A. Pentland. Recognition by parts. In *Proc. of IEEE Conference on Computer Vision*, pages 612–620, London, 1987.

[135] R. Bajcsy, F. Solina. Three dimensional object representation revisited. In *Proc. of IEEE Conference on Computer Vision*, pages 231–240, June 1987.

[136] F. Solina, R. Bajcsy. Recovery of parametric models from range images: The case for superquadrics with global deformations. *IEEE Transactions on Pattern Analysis and Machine Intelligence*, 12(2), 1990.

[137] D. Terzopoulos, D. Metaxas. Dynamic 3d models with local and global deformations: Deformable superquadrics. *IEEE Transactions on Pattern Analysis and Machine Intelligence*, 13(7):703–714, 1991.

[138] W.H. Press, S.A. Teukolsky, W.T. Vetterling, B.P. Flannery. *Numerical Recipes in C*. Cambridge University Press, 2nd edition, 1992.

[139] H. Delingette, M.H.K. Ikeuchi. Shape representation and image segmentation using deformable surfaces. *Image and Vision Computing*, 10(3), 1992.

[140] I. Cohen, L.D. Cohen, N. Ayache. Using deformable surfaces to segment 3-D images and infer differential structures. *Computer Vision, Graphics, and Image Processing*, 56(2):242–263, 1992.

[141] B. Horowitz, A. Pentland. Recovery of non-rigid motion and structure. In *IEEE Computer Society Conference on Computer Vision and Pattern –Recognition (CVPR)*, pages 325–330, 1991.

[142] M. Kass, A. Witkin, D. Terzopoulos. Snakes: Active contour models. In *Proc. of IEEE Conference on Computer Vision*, pages 259–268, London, UK, Jun 8-11 1987.

[143] D.L.G. Hill, D.J. Hawkes. Medical image registration using knowledge of adjacency of anatomical structures. In J. Illingworth, editor, *British machine vision conference*. BMVA Press, Sept. 1993.

[144] L.G. Brown. A survey of image registration techniques. *ACM computing surveys*, 24(4):325–375, 1992.

[145] P.A. van den Elsen, V.-J.D. Pol, M.A. Viergever. Medical image matching – a review with classification. *IEEE Engineering in medicine and biology*, 12(4):26–39, 1993.

[146] B.K.P. Horn. Closed-form solution of absolute orientation using unit quaternions. *Journal Optical Soc. America*, 4(4):629–642, 1987.

[147] O.D. Faugeras, M. Herbert. The representation, recognition, and locating of 3-d objects. *International Journal of Robotics Research*, 5(3):27–52, 1986.

[148] P.J. Besl, N.D. McKay. A method for registration of 3-D shapes. *IEEE Transactions on Pattern Analysis and Machine Intelligence*, 14(2):239–256, 1992.

[149] W.M. Wells, P. Viola, H. Atsumi, S. Nakajima, R. Kikinis. Multimodal volume registration by maximization of mutual information. *Medical Image Analysis*, 1(1):35–51, 1996.

[150] L.H. Staib, X. Lei. Intermodality 3D medical image registration with global search. In *IEEE Workshop on biomedical image analysis*, Seattle, WA, June 1994.

[151] K.H. Höhne, M. Bomans, M. Reimer, R. Schubert, U. Tiede. A volume-based anatomical atlas. *IEEE Computer Graphics and Applications*, 12(7):72–77, 1992.

[152] A. Watt. *3D Computer Graphics*. Addison-Wesley, 2nd ed. edition, 1993.

[153] M. R. Stytz, G. Frieder, O. Frieder. Three-dimensional medical imaging: Algorithms and computer systems. *ACM Computing Surveys*, 23(4):421–499, 1991.

[154] U. Tiede, K.H. Hoehne, M. Bomans, A. Pommert, M. Riemer, G. Wiebecke. Surface rendering. *IEEE Computer Graphics and Applications*, pages 41–53, 1990.

[155] A. Kaufman. Efficient algorithms for scan-converting 3D polygons. *Computers and Graphics*, 12(2):213–219, 1988.

[156] M. Levoy. Efficient ray tracing of volume data. *ACM Transactions on Graphics*, 9(3):245–261, 1990.

[157] R. Yagel, D. Cohen, A. Kaufman. Normal estimation in 3D space. *The Visual computer*, 8(5–6), 1992.

Index